T0002621

DIAMOND JIM TYLER'S

MINI MAGIC MARVELS

Diamond Jim Tyler

Illustrated by Benjamin Vincent

DOVER PUBLICATIONS
Garden City, New York

Bibliographical Note

Diamond Jim Tyler's Mini Magic Marvels is a new work, first published by Dover Publications in 2021.

Several tricks in this book require the use of matches and knives, and some tricks could potentially cause glass to break. Please exercise caution when performing tricks involving fire and sharp objects.

The tricks in this book are not recommended for children.

Library of Congress Cataloging-in-Publication Data

Names: Tyler, Diamond Jim, author.
Title: Diamond Jim Tyler's mini magic marvels / Diamond Jim Tyler ; illustrated by Benjamin Vincent.
Other titles: Mini magic marvels
Description: Garden City, New York : Dover Publications, 2021. | Summary: "Learn magic tricks that are sure to impress your family and friends—because everyone could use a little magic! Easily accessible for beginners and with much to learn for advanced magicians, this instructional guide walks readers through fun party tricks using everyday objects like money and cell phones, meaning no complicated props are needed. Diamond Jim even teaches you some mind-reading effects, requiring nothing but simple know-how. An invaluable addition to any magician's bookshelf"—Provided by publisher.
Identifiers: LCCN 2020053692 | ISBN 9780486848044 (paperback)
Subjects: LCSH: Magic tricks.
Classification: LCC GV1547 .T945 2021 | DDC 793.8—dc23
LC record available at https://lccn.loc.gov/2020053692

Manufactured in the United States by LSC Communications Book LLC
84804301
www.doverpublications.com

2 4 6 8 10 9 7 5 3 1

2021

DIAMOND
JIM TYLER'S

MINI
MAGIC
MARVELS

CONTENTS

CONTENTS

CONTENTS

INTRODUCTION

Everyone could use a little magic. You do not have to be a magician to know how to do some fun party tricks. The easy-to-do gems found between the covers will make you amazing and unforgettable. No matter what you do for a living, these magic effects will show you how to break the ice with people.

You do not have to spend money on props. Diamond Jim Tyler has meticulously found effects that use common, everyday objects. If you were in a restaurant setting, you could use glassware, napkins, bottles, straws, crayons, matches, and coffee cups. If you are in someone's home, you could use playing cards, newspapers, dominoes, paper clips, dice, pens, and pencils. For some of the tricks, you'll need things that could be carried on your person like rubber bands, money, or a cell phone. Diamond Jim even teaches you some mind-reading effects where you will need nothing other than simple know-how.

If you're a teacher, many of these effects could be used to keep the class's attention, even if it's a virtual classroom. If you're a businessperson, these tricks could make you stand out or help close the deal. If you're a server, these bits of business could help increase your tips. Regardless of whether you profit from these tricks monetarily, they are sure to help you put lots of smiles on people's faces, which is priceless.

DIAMOND JIM TYLER'S

MINI
MAGIC
MARVELS

WATCH PREDICTION

The magician wraps an analog watch in a napkin and asks a server to walk away and set the watch to a random time. The magician writes down a prediction on a piece of paper, folds it, and places it on the table. When the server returns, the chosen time matches the prediction!

SECRET: The server becomes your confidant, unbeknownst to the group. On a small piece of paper, write, "Please set the watch to 7:35. Here are a couple dollars for your time. This will be our little secret. Please act surprised when my prediction is read aloud!"

Place a couple dollars and your note on top of the dinner napkin that rests in your lap. Borrow a watch and wrap it up in the napkin, along with the other secret contents, as you call over the server to help with this mind-reading stunt.

━━ ━ ━━

Most servers find it fun to help a magician. They also enjoy making easy money! However, if the server doesn't comply with your request, be sure to stiff them when the bill comes.

Full of Bull

A magician opens a full can of Red Bull®, and his or her hands are otherwise empty. The magician places a finger over the opening and turns the can upside down. Amazingly, when the magician removes the finger, the liquid inside remains suspended. When the can is passed around for inspection, the secret cannot be discerned.

SECRET: This works because of the structure of the Red Bull can. When placing your thumb on top of the open can, slyly spin the pull tab around to cover the opening. Lock one of the pull tab's corners into the mouth of the can so that it doesn't move from that position. Cover the hole with your finger, and turn the can upside down. When you remove the finger covering the hole, the liquid should remain suspended.

A little bit of the liquid may trickle out of the can, but the majority remains inside. If the can is perpendicular to the floor, the liquid may continue to trickle out. However, if you tilt the end of the can that is opposite the mouth slightly toward the floor, no liquid should pour out. To prove that the can is full or that nothing is covering the mouth, insert a straw, matchsticks, or toothpicks into the opening while the can is upside down, and a little bit of liquid will spill out. Or squeeze the can gently to make a little liquid

come out. To end the magical demonstration, place your thumb over the opening and invert the can right side up. As you turn the can, discreetly spin the pull tab back to its original position. This action takes practice. Once the pull tab is in place, pass around the can for inspection and encourage others to try this impossible feat.

Instead of wasting the precious Red Bull liquid, I recommend drinking it and then refilling the can with water before executing this trick.

Speaking of bull, I was born under Taurus the bull,
and man, was he surprised!

Float a Loan

A bill is borrowed and folded into a "Z" shape across its length. The magician balances the folded bill on his or her thumbs and then miraculously removes one hand. The bill remains balanced on the thumb and appears to be floating!

SECRET: Finger palm a nickel in your right hand. Fold a bill. While balancing the bill on your thumbs, discreetly load the nickel onto the bottom portion of the bill. Act as if you are finding the balance, and then remove your left hand altogether. The coin acts as a counterbalance, and from the audience's point of view, this looks amazing!

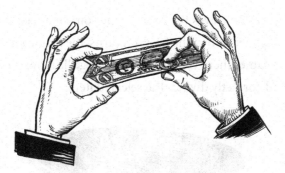

Allow the coin to fall into your right hand again, and secretly retain it in a finger palm, as shown on the facing page. Now the audience can attempt the trick all night long without any luck. Onlookers may think you have something sticky on your fingers and ask to examine your hands. After handing them the bill, ditch the coin as soon as possible.

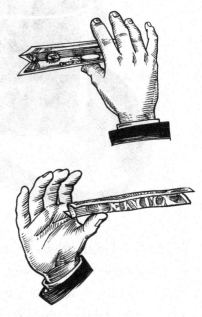

The next time friends ask to borrow some money, you can float them a loan! Yes, I know I am very punny, and my last statement was like a joke without the funny part.

THAT OLE BLACK MAGIC

A psychic friend leaves the room while someone selects an item by pointing to it. When the friend returns, the magician points to things or names them verbally while asking, "Is it this? Is it that?" The friend correctly divines the selected item.

SECRET: Tell your friend in advance that you will point to or name something black and that the next item will be the audience's chosen item. Rehearse it a couple times with your accomplice, and then proceed to freak people out.

I typically don't recommend repeating a trick, but this effect justifies breaking that rule. Audience members may think that you are secretly pointing at the chosen item, so during the next attempt, put your hands in your pocket. Some will think that the chosen item is always in a certain order (e.g., the fifth thing you say). Since that is not the case, let the audience choose which number the chosen item should be. Stop after two or three times so that the audience doesn't become wise to the method. Always leave your audience wanting more!

———

Each time your psychic friend guesses the item correctly, chuckle like a madman to further terrify your audience!

FLOATING BREAD ROLL

The magician covers a bread roll with a cloth napkin. Suddenly, as if the roll has become lighter than air, it begins to float underneath the napkin. Eventually it floats back down to the table, and the roll and napkin can be examined.

SECRET: Prepare the roll by secretly sticking a fork in it at an angle, as shown in the top image. Have the fork and roll ready on the table, while covering both items with a cloth napkin. As you pick up the corners of the napkin, also pick up the fork, as shown in the top image. Allow the roll to bob up slightly above the napkin without exposing the fork, as shown in the second image. Then allow the roll to lower to the center of the napkin, and pretend that it is trying to float away while under the cover of the napkin, as shown in the bottom image. You'll need to do your best pantomiming here. Repeat the "bobbing up over the napkin" and "floating under the center of the napkin" actions a couple times before allowing it to come to a rest near the edge of the table. As it apparently floats back down toward the edge of the table, dislodge the fork from the roll and allow the fork to fall quietly into your lap. Now everyone can examine the napkin and roll.

You could talk about how the yeast in the bread causes it to rise. You could pretend that the roll is possessed by spirits from the great beyond. Or you could pretend that your own power is causing the roll to float and start your own religion.

━━ ▭ ━━

I simply do the trick and say, "You people should all be glad that I use my powers for good!"

Bending Business Card

The magician takes out a business card, folds it into fourths, and holds it as shown in the second image. Upon his or her command, the card bends backward and forward. A mark tries but discovers that this feat is impossible.

SECRET: Prepare a business card by cutting a slit in it, as in the top image. When you remove the business card from a wallet or pocket, be sure to hide that it has been cut. Fold the prepared card into fourths. Hold the card with the slit portion hidden behind the fingers, as in the second image. Using the thumb of the hand holding the card, make the card bend toward you by pulling the thumb down, or make the card bend toward your audience by pushing up with your thumb. The action of pulling down or pushing up should be done very slowly and ever so slightly.

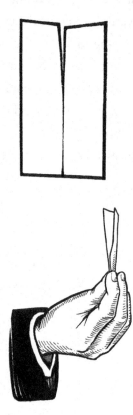

The beautiful thing about this trick is that nearly every angle looks good and does not expose the method. The only bad angle is if someone has a broadside view of the cut portion of the card. I typically use my other hand to misdirect attention and pretend that I am willing the card to move back and forth, as shown in the final image. When you're done, put the card in your pocket and say, "Oh, wait a minute! Perhaps you'd like to try it." Then take out a normal business card that has been folded into fourths, and hand it to the mark.

The victim will try it to no avail. This is a sneaky way of making someone want your business card.

As I walk away, I say, "Hold on to that card because one day it will be worthless. Sooner than you think!"

MENTAL CRAYONS

The magician divines the color of a crayon held behind his back!

Many restaurants stock crayons to keep children entertained. Why should kids have all the fun? Hand someone three or more crayons contrasting in color. Ask the person to hand you one crayon when you are facing away. Say that you will name the color without looking at it. Instruct the person to hide the other crayons behind his or her back or put them in a pocket.

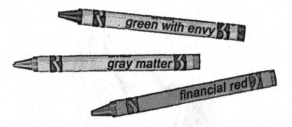

SECRET: Turn back around, and face your audience. While your hands are held behind your back, secretly scrape some of the crayon underneath one of your thumbnails. Bring that same hand out and gesture with it as you make a statement or give instructions. During the moment when your hand is visible, peek at the color underneath your thumbnail and then immediately place that hand behind your back.

When your hand returns behind your back, scrape the crayon out from underneath your nail to remove any trace of the method. I pretend to use my nose and smell the crayon held behind my back. If it is red, I act as if I can smell cherries or strawberries. With a little showmanship, most people forget about your hand coming out from behind your back—which will leave them with no trace of how you did it.

— □ □ □

Remember Mr. Miyagi's advice from The Karate Kid:
"Wax on. Wax off."

CARTESIAN CATSUP

A small ketchup packet is placed inside an enclosed plastic bottle that is filled with water. Upon the magician's command, the ketchup packet sinks to the bottom of the bottle and then floats back to the top. The magician can even cause the ketchup packet to remain suspended in the middle of the bottle.

This scientific stunt is called the Cartesian diver. In the old days, it was done with a glass bottle filled with water, a medicine dropper, and a cork. Once the medicine dropper was placed inside and the bottle was sealed with the cork, all one had to do was place pressure on the cork to cause the dropper to float up and down inside the bottle.

SECRET: I love spins on an old classic, and this is a good one. Place a sealed, small ketchup packet inside a plastic bottle filled with water, and then put the lid on tightly. It is important that the bottle be completely filled. Squeeze the bottle to make the packet sink down to the bottom of the bottle. When the pressure is released, the packet floats to the top.

With practice, you can cause the packet to float up or down to any position in the bottle. The squeezing action should be done covertly. Hold the bottle as shown. If it doesn't work, try a different ketchup packet.

Here's a little joke paraphrased from one of my favorite movies, Quentin Tarantino's Pulp Fiction:
"One day three tomatoes were walking down the street: a mama tomato, a daddy tomato, and a baby tomato. The baby tomato was walking too slowly, so the daddy tomato went back, stepped on him, and said, 'Ketchup!'"

Appearing Straw

The magician rolls up his or her sleeves and shows the front and back of his or her hands. The magician makes a fist with the left hand and magically pulls a drinking straw from it with the right hand.

This looks amazing, but the secret method is a little noisy. Luckily most restaurants and bars are noisy, so the ambient chatter in the background should muffle the slight noise made from this effect.

SECRET: Slyly obtain one of the restaurant's plastic straws, and make your way to the bathroom. While in the bathroom, remove the paper from the straw and slit it along its length with something sharp like a knife or scissors, as shown above. Don't use a clear straw; try to find one that is colored or, better yet, the kind with stripes. Make the cut one long straight line if possible. Roll up the straw, as shown in the second image.

Walk out of the bathroom, and approach your table with the rolled-up straw concealed between the first finger and thumb of your left hand, as shown in the third image. If you keep the two fingers pinched tightly around the straw, you can make it look like both of your hands are empty. When you are ready to have it appear, make a fist with your left hand. Grab one end with your right hand and slowly, but dramatically, pull it from your left fist, as shown in the fourth image. This looks really cool!

If you take a few straws, you can prepare them in the privacy of your own home. Wrap rubber bands around them to keep them wound up, and throw them in your pocket when you are ready for a night out on the town.

Just hope that the rubber bands don't come loose in your pocket, or you may wind up hurting yourself and speaking in high-pitched tones!

Voodoo Blister

The magician traces his or her hand on a piece of paper and asks someone to light a match, blow it out, and touch it to one of the fingers drawn on the paper. The magician then places a hand back on the paper. The magician flinches and gasps as he or she turns the hand over to show that there is a blister on the same finger that was chosen at random.

This is an old trick, but my method is slightly different. Typically, you must hide a device in your hand that has a small, round divot in it. Special rings or keys with holes in them were sometimes used. My method requires that the magician wears a belt, as most of us already do.

SECRET: After tracing your hand on a piece of paper, place both of your thumbs on your pants or fold your arms across your stomach in a relaxed position. As you ask someone to hold the blown-out match to the tip of one of the fingers on the paper, place the tip of the corresponding finger over one of the holes in your belt. Firmly press that fingertip into the hole for three or four seconds. This creates what truly looks like a blister. Hold the same hand to the paper once again, and grimace just before showing everyone the magical, strange occurrence.

If your audience becomes frightened by your magical powers, spread the hairs on the back of your head to reveal that you are not the spawn of the devil!

Fingertip Printing

The magician shows both sides of a pen or pencil, with no writing on either side. Magically, a company's name appears printed on one side of the pen or pencil, and then to your audience's surprise, the words appear on both sides. When the trick is over, the writing instrument has writing on only one side and can be passed around for examination.

SECRET: I prefer to use a No. 2 pencil or a Bic® pen, but just about any writing instrument that has printing on one side can be used. When presenting the pencil, hold it in either hand, with the point toward you and the blank side up. Position it at your fingertips, as shown in the first image. Point the eraser end of the pencil toward the floor.

To show both sides as blank, turn your wrist upward, pointing the end of the pencil toward the ceiling. Secretly roll the pencil toward the end of your fingertips to display the same blank side, as shown on the facing page. This is called the paddle move. Turn your wrist back down, and execute the paddle move again. This should convince everyone that the pencil has no writing on either side.

As you run the other hand's fingers along the length of the pencil, execute the paddle move. It looks as if whatever is imprinted on the pencil just magically appears. Use your empty hand's index finger to rub the imprinted side, and then rub the blank side of the pencil without showing it. Then execute the paddle move to show writing on both sides.

Pretend to erase one side with your fingertip, and then pass around the pencil for inspection. Do not overuse the paddle move during your presentation, or it will make your actions suspicious. This is a terrific trick because you can borrow a normal writing instrument and perform a minor miracle with it. One could also have pens or pencils imprinted with their own information, perform the trick, and leave spectators with a souvenir that they are not likely to forget or throw away!

Conclude with some thought-provoking words by saying,
"My mom always told me that I was unique,
just like everyone else!"

Magnetic Coins

Rub two quarters on your sleeve, and show that they are now magnetized!

SECRET: Rubbing the coins against your sleeve is a ploy to throw the audience off track. To make it appear as if the quarters are magnetic, hold the first quarter firmly with your left thumb and index finger, as shown above. Hold the second quarter with your right thumb and index finger in the same position, but use a loose grip. Press the quarter in your right hand onto the tip of your left thumb until it clicks onto the quarter held by your left hand, as shown in the second image.

The illusion of the coins clicking together makes them appear to be magnetic. As you pull back the quarter held by your right hand with a light grip,

allow the edge of the coin to catch underneath the tip of your left thumb, which should hold its coin with a firm grip. As you pull back the coin in the right hand, it snaps back as if it were magnetically attached to the other coin, as shown below.

The position of your left thumb is important because it should remain hidden behind the quarter. A quarter is the smallest coin that you should perform this trick with because your thumb must remain shielded. When using a bigger coin like a half-dollar or a silver dollar, the illusion is stronger because the larger metal surface area produces a louder clanking noise.

―――

To explain this amazing feat, state,
"It must be my magnetic personality. I'm positive that
I attract negative energy toward myself and that I can
repel anyone with an iron constitution."

Houdini Rubber Band

A rubber band visually penetrates the magician's fingers.

SECRET: Place a rubber band over your first two right fingers. Pull it toward your right wrist with your left fingers, as shown above. Curl all of your right fingers into a closed fist, putting them inside the rubber band, as shown in the second image. Release the rubber band so that it snaps back just under your right hand's first knuckles. Cover the previous maneuver with what magicians call "misdirection." To misdirect the audience during this effect, talk about the famous Harry Houdini and how he was known for escaping from locked chains, handcuffs, boxes, jail cells, and straitjackets.

Show the audience the back of your hand and the rubber band wrapped around your fingers, as shown in the third image. Straighten or uncurl your fingers, and the rubber band jumps onto your third and fourth fingers, as shown in the final image. From the audience's perspective, it looks as if the rubber band has penetrated your fingers. This happens so fast that sometimes the audience misses what happens. Sometimes I repeat the action and cause the rubber band to jump back to the other side. Use your best judgment.

Find a brightly colored rubber band, if possible. Use a rubber band that just fits over two of your fingers when it's in a relaxed state. Do not employ a rubber band that is too big or too small.

═ ═ □ ═ ═

This is such a great effect that magician David Copperfield has used it on some of his television specials. I am proud of David. He turned out to be one of my better students!

Karate Dollar

While someone holds on to a crayon, a folded dollar bill is thrust toward it and snaps the crayon in two!

SECRET: Your index finger breaks the crayon in two. However, the audience will believe that the dollar performed this miracle. The dollar bill should be folded in half along its width. Ask someone to hold on to a crayon, with one end in each hand. Grip one end of the folded bill with your thumb and your index finger's knuckle. Raise the same arm into the air. Lower your arm quickly while striking the crease of the folded bill against the center of the crayon.

This is done a couple times to condition all who are watching. When you are ready to snap the crayon into two pieces, outstretch your index finger as you quickly bring your arm and hand down. The dollar bill shields your outstretched finger. Hit the center of the crayon with the side of your finger. As soon as the crayon snaps in two, retract your index finger back into your closed fist. Once you've mastered breaking crayons, you can move on to breaking pencils.

———

If you enjoyed this trick, then you might like origami, the Japanese art of paper folding. I once knew a guy who had a black belt in origami. When he got mad, he'd give people paper cuts!

Spoon Bending

The magician appears to bend a spoon in front of an audience. Then to everyone's surprise, the spoon straightens itself!

SECRET: You need a metal spoon and a nickel. Secretly retain the nickel in your left hand between your first finger and your thumb. Pick up a spoon in your right hand and hold the handle between your middle finger and pinky, with your thumb on top, as shown in the first image. Place your left hand on top of your right hand, and allow the end of the handle of the spoon to push the nickel slightly out of your left hand's cupped position, as shown in the second image. If you don't allow too much of the nickel to show, your audience will believe it to be the end of the spoon's handle. Keeping your hands in the same position, bring them down forcefully on the table, as shown in the final image. The spoon pivots in your hand, but the illusion suggests that you have bent the spoon.

The thing that convinces the audience the most is your facial expressions and the noises you make. Act as if the spoon is tough to bend. Grunt while you are bending it. Exhale once you've done it. Pause for a moment, and then allow the nickel to fall back inside your left hand. While concealing the nickel, pretend to bend the spoon back to normal, just before handing it out for inspection.

———

As your audience examines the spoon, ask, "Hey, do you know where I can get some mice?" As people respond and look at you funny, flex your muscles and kiss your biceps as you proclaim, "Because these pythons are hungry!"

Magic Spinning Coin

The magician stands a coin on the table and holds it upright by placing a finger on top of it. With his or her other hand, the magician rubs the finger vigorously. Eventually the coin takes off spinning, as if by magic!

I love quick, little tricks. This trick teaches a valuable lesson to beginning magicians. The principle is that a big motion conceals a little motion.

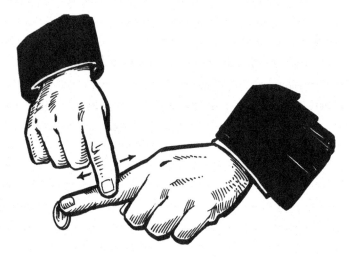

SECRET: Begin by balancing a coin on its rim on the tabletop, with one of the flat sides facing you. Rest your right index finger gently on top of the coin to hold it in position. Stroke your right index finger with the tip of your left index finger several times, as if you are creating kinetic energy, as shown above. The remaining fingers of the left hand should be curled in toward the palm, except for the thumb, which should remain outstretched.

Repeat the same rubbing action with your left hand, but move your thumb in closer so that it can strike the coin on its side and cause it to spin, as shown below. As soon as the coin takes off, separate your hands and focus your attention on the spinning coin.

Like most good tricks, this one should not be repeated for the same group. If someone asks you to do it again, say, "Good magicians don't repeat their tricks . . . and neither do I."

SWEET MAGIC

The magician plucks a sugar packet out of the holder in the center of the table. The magician rips off the top of the packet and pours the contents into his or her closed fist. Upon command, the sugar completely vanishes!

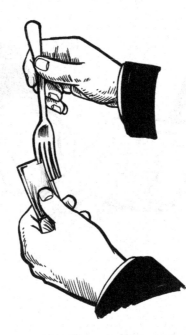

SECRET: Prepare one of the sugar packets in advance. Use the prong of a fork to poke a hole in one corner of a packet, as shown above. Shake the sugar out of the packet, and secretly place the packet back in the holder. Sometimes when presenting this effect, I palm the empty packet in my hand and mimic the action of taking it out of the packet holder as I say, "Hey, everybody! Check this out!"

When executing the effect, tear off the top piece with the hole and discard it. Squeeze the packet open so that it looks full. Hold the open mouth of the packet close to your fist as you pretend to pour the contents into your fist, as shown in the second image. Leave a little sugar in the packet so people can see some of it collect on top of your fist. Brush off the little bit that remains on top of your closed fist, and say a magic word. Open your hand to reveal that the sweetener has vanished!

Use any magic word that speaks to you. I like "Shammalamma-ding-dong!"

CALLING MR. WIZARD

The magician claims that a friend, Mr. Wizard, can read minds. He or she asks someone to select a card and show it to everyone or simply name a card out loud. The magician calls Mr. Wizard and hands the phone to the spectator. Unbelievably, Mr. Wizard divines the card correctly!

SECRET: This is a classic in magic. The person who plays Mr. Wizard is a confederate. You can have someone select a card or merely think of one. It is important that you know what the card is. Once you do, call your confederate and do the following.

When the confederate answers the phone, say, "Hello, Mr. Wizard?" This signals that he should begin slowly reciting the numbers in a deck of cards: "ace, two, three, four . . . ." When the confederate reaches the correct number, say, "He says that he knew I was about to call him!" This makes everyone laugh and cues him to what the number is.

The confederate then recites the card suits—"clubs, hearts, spades . . ."—until you interrupt him again, which tells him the suit. Typically, I interrupt Mr. Wizard by saying, "He'd like to speak with you." Hand the phone to the person thinking of the card. Mr. Wizard then reveals the card. The miraculous prediction usually becomes apparent to the rest of the crowd when the spectator reacts to Mr. Wizard's revelation.

If you perform this trick impromptu, then do it as described. If you know something about one of the people attending the gathering, give Mr. Wizard some insight beforehand. If you don't know anyone there, you could still call Mr. Wizard shortly before performing the stunt and tell him what the spectator's name is or what he or she looks like or is wearing. With this firsthand knowledge, Mr. Wizard can blow the person's mind!

When this trick is executed flawlessly, it can really scare people. Set it up with a few friends, so that when the opportunity arises, you can catch Mr. Wizard on the phone.

I have always wished that I could read minds. This past Christmas I asked for a crystal ball, but my parents said there was no future in it.

Invisible Dice

The volunteer rolls invisible dice. After doing what seems like random math, the magician divines the numbers that the volunteer rolled!

The magician hands someone a pair of invisible dice. The magician asks that he or she roll the dice and inquires, "What number did you roll?" After the volunteer responds, the magician insists, "Roll them again." After he or she complies, the magician asks, "What number did you get this time?" After responding with a different number, the magician proclaims, "So they are not loaded!" Everyone chuckles.

The magician asks that the person roll the dice one last time. The magician adds, "This time, don't tell me what you rolled. Instead choose one of the two numbers that you rolled and double it. Now add five to your new number. Multiply the result by five, and add the number on the other die to it. What is your new total?" After hearing the response, the magician astonishes everyone by revealing the numbers that the volunteer rolled. The magician adds, "Do you know how I guessed your numbers? It was easy. You left the dice sitting on the table."

SECRET: The real method uses a little math. Let's say the volunteer rolled a 5 and a 2.

If he or she chooses the 5 and doubles it, that makes 10.

Adding 5 to 10 makes 15.

Multiplying 15 by 5 equals 75.

Adding the other number, 2, to that total is 77.

The secret is to subtract 25 from this last total!

77 minus 25 equals 52. The result 52 indicates that the person rolled a 5 and a 2.

$$\boxed{\vcenter{\hbox{⚄}}} \, \& \, \boxed{\vcenter{\hbox{⚁}}}$$

$$\boxed{\vcenter{\hbox{⚄}}} \times 2 = 10$$

$$10 + 5 = 15$$

$$15 \times 5 = 75$$

$$75 + \boxed{\vcenter{\hbox{⚁}}} = 77$$

$$77 - 25 = 52$$

$$52 = \boxed{\vcenter{\hbox{⚄}}} \, \& \, \boxed{\vcenter{\hbox{⚁}}}$$

This always works. It is amazing! If you decide to try this on an elementary school student, someone who has been drinking, or someone who just doesn't seem that bright, hand the person a pencil and paper or a calculator to work out the calculations.

━━ ▭ ━━

If there's one thing I've learned over the years, it is that there are three kinds of people. There are those who can count and those who can't.

MOODY DOLLAR

The president's portrait on a dollar bill is made to smile and frown.

SECRET: Crease the bill on each side of the president's mouth, as shown above. Then make a valley fold between the two creases, as shown below. Stretch out the bill, and stare into the president's eyes.

When you tilt the bill forward, the president seems to frown. When you tilt the bill backward, the president seems to smile. It's truly amazing! Plus, it works with every bill denomination.

Typically, I do this trick with a borrowed bill so that I can leave people with a neat souvenir. However, you do have the option of sticking the bill in your pocket and running out the door.

Telekinetic Straw

The magician removes a straw from its wrapper and balances it on top of a ketchup bottle. The magician points at the straw, and it begins to move. Whichever way the magician beckons the straw to move, it does so. The audience can examine the straw and try to do the trick but will not discover the method.

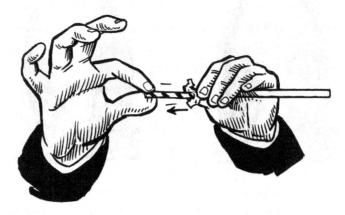

SECRET: You are using the power of static electricity. Remove one end of the wrapper from a plastic straw. Pinch the open end of the wrapper and straw between your left index finger and thumb. Pull the straw free from the wrapper with your right hand while keeping the same pinched grip with your left hand, as shown above. This pinched grip puts a static charge in the straw.

Do not let go of the straw with your right hand until you balance the center of the straw on top of the closed ketchup bottle. If you grip the straw again or release the pinched grip, the straw may lose its static charge. Once the straw is balanced on the bottle, put your outstretched index finger close to one end of the straw. The static charge attracts it toward your finger, as shown below. Typically, I cause the straw to go one way and then put my finger on the other side of the straw to make it stop and go in the opposite direction.

This action looks magical! I do it a few times before grabbing the straw, handing it to someone, and saying, "Check it out!" When you grab the straw, you break the static charge, thus making the straw examinable. If people mimic your actions, they will fail. Another way to put a static charge in the drinking straw is to run it vigorously through your hair, but I prefer the pinched wrapper method.

When your audience looks at you in wonder, say, "If you believe in the power of telekinesis, then raise my hand."

Phoenix Ashes

The magician rubs ash on the back of a spectator's closed fist. Miraculously, upon opening the fist, the spectator discovers ash on his or her palm.

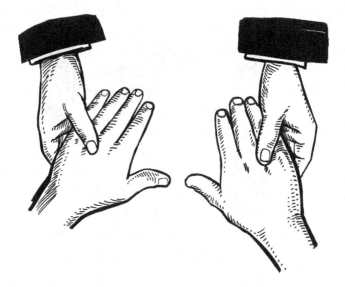

SECRET: When no one is looking, stick the middle finger of your right hand into an ashtray and smear some ash on it. I use the Criss Angel method. I point toward the door and say, "Look! There's Criss Angel!" Then I quickly put the ash on my finger. I'm kidding, of course, but you do want to be sly.

Ask someone to hold out both hands palm-down. Grab both hands with your hands, as shown above, and distract the person by saying, "Hold them both like this." This transfers ash from your middle finger onto his or her left palm. Allow your hands to relax at your side, and keep your dirty middle finger hidden.

Instruct the person, "Make both hands into a fist, and then slowly begin to raise one of them." If the person raises the right fist, then say, "Okay, let's eliminate that hand by letting it relax at your side." If he or she raises the left fist, then say, "Since you want to use your left hand, allow your right hand to relax at your side." You are forcing the person to use the left hand for this trick. This method is known as the magician's choice.

Approach the ashtray on the table with your right hand, and dip your middle finger in it to collect some ash. This action conceals the fact that there was already ash on the finger. Put a little ash on the back of the person's left fist with your right hand. Using your left hand, rub the ash into the skin until it is no longer visible.

Ask if anyone has ever heard of the Egyptian myth of the phoenix. Explain, "The bird symbolized death and rebirth. It was said to die in a blaze of fire, but then it would be born again from its own ashes." As I say this, I light a match, blow it out, and place it directly under the spectator's left fist to allow the smoke to billow up toward his or her hand. Ask the person to open his or her left hand and turn his or her palm up. The spectator's eyes will bulge upon seeing the ashes on his or her palm.

As the audience freaks out, ask,
"Where do you think I should build my church?"

DICE CUBES

Have someone drop three dice in a glass of water. Ask the person to add up the sum of the bottoms of the dice. The magician then holds a hand over the glass, turns away, and concentrates. Amazingly, the magician reveals the sum as if by osmosis.

SECRET: All regulation dice abide by the "rule of seven": Opposite sides of a die always equal seven. The number six is back-to-back with the number one. The number five is back-to-back with the number two. And the number four is back-to-back with the number three.

Since you are using three dice, multiply the "rule of seven" by three, making the magic number twenty-one. If you subtract the sum of the numbers on the tops of the dice from twenty-one, you get the sum of the numbers on the bottoms. For example, 21 - 12 = 9.

While your audience is busy adding the numbers on the bottoms of the dice, secretly glance at the top numbers. Once the audience is done, act as if the sum is coming to you telepathically and reveal it.

See! Math class paid off after all. Now, as for geometry, that was a waste of time.

Newspaper Prediction

The magician cuts a column from a borrowed newspaper and writes down a prediction on a piece of paper. The paper is folded and placed in plain sight. The magician runs a pair of scissors up and down the column and asks a volunteer to say "stop" at any time. When the volunteer says "stop," the magician cuts the paper and allows it to flutter to the floor. When the volunteer reads the line where the paper was cut, it matches the magician's prediction.

This is a great effect that can be performed impromptu so long as you have a newspaper and scissors. The method is so simple that I laugh inside when performing the trick. However, there are a few things you must do to pull off this miracle.

SECRET: For the sake of giving your audience more to choose from, cut the longest possible single-strip column from a newspaper. Be sure that the font on the paper is the same size. A large headline or a picture would expose the method. Stand back from your audience about two arm's lengths or at least six feet. And here's the secret: Turn the strip upside down!

When you cut the strip from the newspaper, note the top line and make it your prediction. When you stand back and hold the strip upside down, no one will notice. Run the scissors up and down the strip and cut the strip when the person says "Stop." When he or she picks up the strip from the floor to read the top line, it will match your prediction.

What if the person picks up the strip from the floor and reads the wrong side? That is even better. I ask the person to read my prediction aloud. Most audiences sigh and show a little sympathy at your failed attempt. If they are like my friends, they ridicule you. Regardless of their reaction, ask the person to read the other side of the strip aloud. When they realize you've succeeded, all will bow at your feet. Wad up the remaining part of the leftover strip, and discard it to destroy the evidence.

——— —— ———

Ask everyone, "Do you believe in ESP?"
Regardless of their replies, follow up by saying,
"What about ESPN, the Psychic Sports Network?"

CUP OF MOJO

Ask someone to draw something on the back of a business card and place it with the drawing facing down on the table. The magician picks it up momentarily and folds it into fourths. The magician concentrates and slowly reveals what was drawn!

SECRET: The next time you want to amaze your friends in a restaurant, order your coffee black. If you take cream, only add it after performing this trick. Ask your friend to draw something on a business card like a number, a letter, or a simple picture while your back is turned. Ask the friend to place the card with the drawing facing down on the table.

Pick up the business card and say, "There is no way to see through the paper or know what it is you have drawn." When picking up the card, angle what was drawn over the full cup of coffee, as shown above. Look into your cup briefly, and you will see a reflection of what was drawn. Fold the card into fourths, and then slowly divulge the hidden message.

Practice the above action so that it isn't too obvious. If you and your cup of joe are positioned correctly, the rest of your audience should not be able to see the reflection. Once you've performed this trick a few times, you'll know exactly how far the card needs to be from the cup to pull it off. This is another sneaky way to make someone want to keep your business card.

———— ▬ ————

I conclude by saying, "I'd tell you some of my Nostradamus jokes, but you wouldn't get them for another 100 years."

THE DOMINO EFFECT

The magician presents an ordinary set of dominoes and places them all on the table with the number side up. The magician asks a volunteer to connect the dominoes in numerical order as if someone were playing the game. The magician predicts the numbers at each end of the long line of dominoes. Believe it or not, the magician can repeat the effect and predict a different outcome each time.

All you need is a regulation set of "double six" dominoes and something to write your prediction on. The only stipulation is that it must be a full set of twenty-eight dominoes.

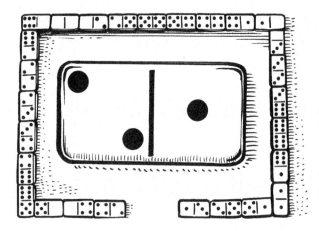

SECRET: As you mix the dominoes by scattering them across the tabletop, secretly palm one or slyly slide it off the table into your lap. Sneak a peek at the numbers that appear on this hidden domino, and you'll have your prediction. For example, if you palm off the domino with one and two, then when the volunteer finishes lining up all the dominoes, the numbers on each end will be one and two.

Make your prediction before your volunteer begins lining up the dominoes. If you have never played dominoes and are not sure how to line them up properly, look at the picture provided. Stress that the outcome is unforeseeable because you have no idea which domino the volunteer will choose or how they will be aligned. This is somewhat of a lie. If the volunteer uses all the dominoes—which you must insist on—the outcome is predictable. The simple fact is that most people, even serious domino players, don't know this.

When the trick is over, secretly add the domino that was in your lap back into the mix of dominoes on the table as you begin shuffling them again. You could palm off a different domino, repeat the trick, and show everyone that the outcome is always different. The only problem with this trick is finding a set of dominoes.

The next time you find yourself at a Shriners,
Knights of Columbus, or Kiwanis meeting, you could
borrow their dominoes and knock 'em dead.
Well . . . I wouldn't go that far!

Sudoku Savant

The spectator picks a number between 22 and 100. The magician fills out a four-by-four grid where every row and column—up and down, across, and diagonally—plus some other combinations add up to the designated number. The magician does this in mere seconds!

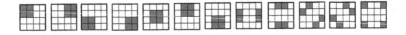

SECRET: This trick is better known as a magic square. Provided below are templates that allow you to pull this off. Let's say the spectator picks 37. Whatever number is given to you, subtract 21 from it. In the left figure below, place the result in the box marked A. Then add 1 to that number, and put it in box B. Add 1 to that, and put it in box C. Add 1 to that, and put it in box D. The other numbers in the grid are always the same. Whatever number the spectator gives you, the grid adds up in every vertical column and horizontal and diagonal row, plus many other ways, as shown in the small boxes above.

Ⓑ	1	12	7
11	8	Ⓐ	2
5	10	3	Ⓓ
4	Ⓒ	6	9

17	1	12	7
11	8	16	2
5	10	3	19
4	18	6	9

Ask that the spectator give you a number between 1 and 100. For the sake of the math involved, it is best that the number be between 30 and 60. Any number higher than 21 works. Once the person gives you the number, subtract 21 from it and fill in boxes A, B, C and D. Then fill in the other numbers. In order not to spoil the surprise, do not reveal your drawing until you are finished.

You could memorize the sequence, or you could just make a copy of the left figure and hide it as a crib sheet. I usually print it on a tiny piece of paper and tape it to a marker so that I can refer to the numbers.

When people see all the different ways that the grid adds up to the designated number, they will think you are a savant. If you'd like to perform this as a mind-reading stunt, simply fill in the twelve numbers that are always the same as you ask the spectator to think of a number. Then ask for the number; fill in boxes A, B, C, and D; and blow their minds.

When your bewildered audience looks to you for a plausible explanation, say, "Hey! I am just like you— only smarter and better-looking."

Magic of the Mind

A spectator is asked to think of a number, a letter, a country, and an animal. Acting as a psychic, you can reveal his or her thoughts!

SECRET: It sounds impossible, but this actually works. The method relies on math. When giving the following instructions, ask the spectator to think of the first thing that comes to mind when choosing items at random:

1. Think of a number between one and ten.
2. Multiply that number by nine.
3. If it's a two-digit number, add the digits together.
4. Subtract five from the new number.
5. Note the letter that matches the new number (e.g., A = 1, B = 2).
6. Think of a country that starts with this letter.
7. Take the second letter from the country's name.

8. Think of an animal whose name starts with that letter.

9. Think about the color of this animal.

Pretend to be receiving the person's thoughts, and proclaim, "There are no gray elephants in Denmark!" Upon hearing this revelation, most people fall out of their chairs! Step three forces the number nine on the person, and the rest is sheer probability.

Ask someone who claims to be sober,
"How many legs do you see on the elephant?"

Karate Matchbook

The magician tosses a matchbook in the air, screams "Hi-ya!" and penetrates the matchbook in midair with an index finger.

SECRET: You need two identical matchbooks. Prep one by placing a ballpoint pen through its center, penetrating the front and back covers. While the pen is sticking through the matchbook, move it around to expand the hole. Remove the pen, and widen the hole by sticking your index finger through it.

Remove your index finger, and flip open the matchbook cover. Stick four or five of the centermost matches through the hole in the back cover. Close the matchbook cover. When you are ready to impress your audience, place your index finger through the hole so that the prepared matchbook rests on your first knuckle.

This is the perfect after-dinner trick or bar stunt. The best scenario is when someone brings up the subject of strength or speed. Otherwise, bring it up yourself. Turn the topic toward yourself, and say, "I hate to brag, but I'm pretty swift and strong myself." Toss the normal matchbook into the air with your left hand. Scream a guttural karate "Hi-ya!" as you catch the matchbook with your right hand's middle, ring, and pinky fingers.

Keep your right index finger sticking straight out to display the penetrated matchbook. Looking at this head-on, your audience will not be able to see the matchbook hidden in your right hand's grip, as shown on the facing page. When the tossing and catching action is done quickly, the illusion is perfect. The noise made by catching the matchbook sounds as if you penetrated it with your finger. All will be amazed!

There are two great ways to clean up and get rid of the normal matchbook in your right hand. If sitting, bring the heel of your right hand to the table's edge; drop the concealed matchbook into your lap as you remove the punctured matchbook from your right finger with your left hand. If standing, remove the matchbook from your right finger with your left hand and present someone with the penetrated matchbook. As all gaze upon the shredded evidence of your supreme strength, place both hands in your pocket, as if relaxing, and discard the matchbook.

Conclude by saying, "I can tell you people have never seen me before, or you would be a lot more excited right now."

STICKY PENCIL

The magician rubs an ordinary pencil against his or her open palm and, upon stopping, the pencil stays suspended or appears to be stuck to the hand.

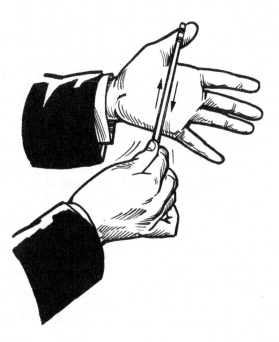

SECRET: Press the pencil firmly into your palm, and vigorously rub it back and forth, as shown above. This causes friction, and the heat creates a chemical reaction between the skin's moisture and the paint on the pencil. Eventually the pencil becomes sticky, and it remains stuck to your hand for a short while.

Open your left hand with the palm facing up, and use your right hand's fingers to press and rub the pencil rapidly against your left palm. Once the pencil is stuck, hold your left hand's open palm and the pencil perpendicular to the floor, as shown below. Place your right hand about eight inches underneath the pencil. Be ready to catch it if it falls. Time the action of twitching the muscles in your left palm and snapping your right hand's fingers so that as you snap your fingers, the pencil falls from your left hand into your right hand.

Before and after the trick, you can allow people to examine the pencil and your hands to see that there is nothing sticky on them.

—— — ——

When they ask how you did it, reply, "The answer is on my website. Go to nunya . . . that's n, u, n, y, a . . . bizness . . . b, i, z, n, e, s, s .com. That's NunyaBizness.com."

Hydrostatic Bottle

The magician inverts a borrowed bottle full of liquid mouth-down, and the contents inside remain suspended. To prove that nothing is covering the opening, the magician inserts matches or toothpicks, and they float up inside the bottle. This looks incredible!

SECRET: This version uses a gimmick, but practically any bottle—water, beer, soda, etc.—can be used. Cut out a circle the size of a quarter from a thick piece of clear plastic. Use a piece of plastic that's thick enough to hold its shape and remain flat, such as the type that snugly fits around items in retail stores. Try to find some plastic that is clear and thick, like a piece of laminate.

After cutting out a circle, light a wooden match, blow it out, and place the head of the hot match through the center of the clear disk over and over. This makes a small hole that is slightly larger than the circumference of the head of the match. Place this small prepared disk in your wallet, and you are set to perform this trick seemingly impromptu.

If you know exactly what kind of bottle you'll perform this trick with, trace the mouth of the bottle on the clear plastic, cut it out, and prepare a disk that fits precisely.

PERFORMANCE: Finger-palm the doughnutlike disk in your right hand, as shown on the facing page, and grab the full bottle with your left hand. While covering the opening of the bottle with your right hand's fingers, align the disk over the mouth and apply a little pressure. Invert the bottle upside down, and carefully remove your fingers. The disk should cling to the mouth of the bottle. This in and of itself looks incredible since the liquid remains suspended.

The mouth of the bottle is pointed toward the floor and is away from your audience's line of sight so that the disk remains undetected. If the audience doesn't believe it to be real magic, then some may make the logical leap that something is covering the opening. To disprove that, insert matchsticks or toothpicks into the opening. If you push a toothpick less than halfway through the hole in the disk and let go, it should remain dangling there, as shown on the next page. Give the toothpick a little tap, and it will float up to the top of the liquid inside the bottle.

After putting a few matchsticks or toothpicks in the bottle and performing this little miracle for less than a minute, cup your right hand's fingers over the opening in the bottle. Turn the

bottle right side up, and finger-palm the disk again. Hand someone the bottle to inspect, or simply place it on the table with your left hand. The disk is easily ditched so that your hands can be examined as well.

If you perform this trick outside over dirt, grass, or concrete with a bottle of water, squeeze the bottle firmly or strike the bottom of the bottle while it is upside down so that the audience can witness everything rushing out of the bottle. The disk will be camouflaged on the ground. While bending down to pick up the matchsticks or toothpicks, try to obtain the disk discreetly so that you can reuse it.

Did you know that connoisseurs of bottled water prefer Evian®? But then again, Evian spelled backwards is naive.

VINO MAGNIFICO

Balance a full glass of wine on the edge of a plate.

SECRET: See the image above. Obviously, when you perform this stunt, your audience should be in front of you. Pretend that you are finding the center of gravity or having difficulty balancing the wine glass at first. Let the glass rest on the plate for a moment, with your thumb secretly helping, before removing the glass. If this is done quickly, no one can guess the method. Practice and perfect this stunt before trying it, especially if using a full glass of wine.

— — —

When I am at parties, people often bring their kids up to me and ask if I can show or teach them a trick. After I perform this stunt, I say, "Be sure to practice this one when mommy and daddy aren't home."

Out to Lunch

Get a free meal with some business cards, a pen, and a rubber band.

SECRET: There is a little preparation involved. Make a small stack of six to ten of your business cards. All the cards should face the same direction, with the blank side showing. Print your friend's name (e.g., Bob) on the top of the backmost card. Cut one business card in half, as shown above. Place one of the half cards, with the blank side showing, over Bob's name to conceal it. Align the cards, and wrap a short, fat rubber band around the center of the business cards to hold the half card in place, as shown on the next page. This principle is known to the magic community as "Out to Lunch," created by Edward Bagshawe in 1930.

You are ready to win a free meal if you can sucker your friend into this. Put the prepared cards in your pocket. After lunch, pull out the cards and write your name on the half card. Write "buys lunch" under the rubber band. The illusion makes it look as if everything is written on the same card. Turn the rubber-banded cards and your message down, and carefully pull out the bottommost card. Place this card message side down on the table. The card reads "Bob buys lunch."

Pull out another business card from under the rubber band, being careful not to let the half card come loose. Write "Bob buys lunch" on the back of the card, and turn it message-side down. Place the rubber-banded cards in your pocket to hide the half card with your name on it. Mix up the cards, and allow your friend to do so as well. When your friend turns over the card, say, "All right! Today is my lucky day!"

Place the other business card with your friend's name on it in your pocket. Pray that your friend doesn't ask to see it. If he or she does, you could have another one printed out with your name on it and switch out the cards.

If you face the moral dilemma of cheating your friends,
then have lunch with an enemy.

CALLING MR. WIZARD #2

The magician claims that his or her friend Mr. Wizard can read minds. The magician asks someone to select a card and show it to everyone or name the card out loud. The magician calls Mr. Wizard and hands the phone to the spectator. Unbelievably, Mr. Wizard divines the card correctly!

After a card is named, say the two of clubs, the magician pulls out a business card from a wallet to find a phone number for Mr. Wizard. The magician reads the number off the card and calls him. The magician says, "Hello, Blake. I mean Mr. Wizard. This is Diamond Jim calling on behalf of a friend who'd like to speak to you." When you call your friend Blake, you clue him in as to what the selection is. Hand the spectator the phone, and instruct him or her to ask Mr. Wizard what the card is. After receiving his psychic vibrations, Mr. Wizard reveals the card.

CLUBS	SPADES
A- Bob	A- James
2- Blake	2- Joe
3- Brendan	3- Jack
4- Brandon	4- Jimmy
5- Brian	5- Jerry
6- Bryce	6- Jason
7- Bill	7- Jesse
8- Barry	8- Jerome
9- Benjamin	9- Jared
10- Brad	10- John
J- Blair	J- Joshua
Q- Brent	Q- Justin
K- Bruce	K- Jacob

HEARTS	DIAMONDS
A- Lane	A- Rick
2- Landen	2- Robert
3- Larry	3- Ray
4- Luke	4- Ross
5- Lance	5- Randy
6- Lee	6- Roger
7- Louis	7- Rex
8- Logan	8- Richard
9- Leland	9- Reed
10- Lyle	10- Ron
J- Leonard	J- Ryan
Q- Lorenzo	Q- Rex
K- Lester	K- Ralph

JOKER-

SECRET: On the business card that you remove from your wallet is the phone number for your psychic friend as well as fifty-three different first names for Mr. Wizard. When you ask for Mr. Wizard, your cohort will know it is not a wrong number. Calling him by one of the first names tells him which card has been chosen. Rather than memorizing all fifty-three names, print all the names on the back of a business card. Mr. Wizard needs a copy of the list as well. Photocopy it, and affix it to a business card. There was a method in my madness when I chose the names.

In case some wise guy picks the joker, have a fail-safe name ready. Make it something inconspicuous like Eggbert Allowicious Von Humperdinck.

Purloined Peanuts

Three random items are placed on a table. While the magician's back is turned, three volunteers each hide an item behind their backs. With the aid of some peanuts, the magician can tell who has each item.

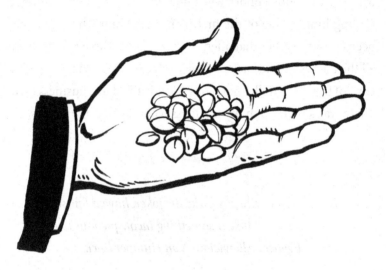

SECRET: This is a mathematical trick that dates back to medieval times. It was made popular by the late, great Martin Gardner. Have three friends produce three random items like a toothpick, a quarter, and a sugar packet. Assign each item a letter (e.g., A = toothpick, B = quarter, C = sugar packet). Envision each item with the letter printed on it. Place the items in the center of the table.

You need twenty-four peanuts. If someone is allergic or peanuts are not available, use Tic Tac® breath mints or M&M's®. Count the edible items before beginning this trick to help mask the fact that you're using math during the effect.

Assign each of the three helpers a number between one and three. Call the person to the left #1, and place one peanut in front of him or her. The person in the middle is #2, who receives two peanuts. The person on the right is #3 and gets three peanuts. This leaves you with eighteen peanuts, which should be left on the table.

The magician turns his or her back and asks each volunteer to take one of the three items and place it behind his or her back. Tell the volunteer who hid item A to take the *same* amount of peanuts that the person has in front of him or her from your pile and eat all of those peanuts. Instruct the volunteer who hid item B to remove *twice* as many peanuts as the person has and eat them. The person who took item C should take *four* times as many peanuts as he or she has and dispose of them.

When the magician turns back around to see the amount of peanuts remaining in his or her own pile, it is clear who has each item. There should be one, two, three, five, six, or seven peanuts remaining. If there are four, something went wrong. Memorize this mnemonic sentence, and you'll know who has which item:

ABhor **BA**d **A**c**ts**; don't **BeC**kon **CA**ddie **CluB**s.

Let's say there are three peanuts remaining. This tells you to recognize the third word in the mnemonic sentence, which is "acts." The word "acts" tells you that person #1 has object A and person #2 has object C, and that leaves person #3 with object B. This is easy once you practice a few times.

Once you see the remaining peanuts, gobble them down. Your volunteers have helped destroy the evidence by devouring their peanuts.

——— — ———

Did you hear the one about the guy sitting alone at the bar? He hears someone say, "Hey, good-looking!" He looks around and sees no one. A few minutes later, he hears, "That's a snazzy shirt you're wearing." He spins around on his stool and discovers no one. A chill runs up his spine. So he calls over the bartender and says, "I keep hearing voices, and no one is around. The weird thing is the ghostly sayings are very flattering. What did you put in my drink?" The bartender laughs and says, "You're not hearing voices, and you are not drunk." The bartender points to a bowl of peanuts in front of the patron and says, "It's the nuts. They're complimentary."

SALTY BEER

Salt magically penetrates the bottom of the magician's mug of beer and floats up to the surface of the drink.

SECRET: Say, "I always like to add a little salt to my beer. And I do it magically." Pick up your full mug in one hand and a saltshaker in the other. Strike the bottom of the mug with the top of the saltshaker. The tiny white gas bubbles that rise from the bottom of the glass look like salt as they float upward, as shown above. Do this a couple times, if you like. An extra subtlety is to wipe away any salt that clings to the bottom of the mug.

It was my uncle who turned me on to salty beer. He drank all kinds of weird concoctions. Once I witnessed him drink a quart of shellac. He died from it . . . but what a finish!

SAFETY PIN SURPRISE

Two safety pins are shown and fastened shut. Both are placed in a spectator's fist. Upon the magician's command, the safety pins are heard and felt to unlink and open in the spectator's hand.

This effect is credited to the late, great genius of the magician Jerry Andrus. Google Mr. Andrus, and you will find a plethora of optical illusions, magic, and more.

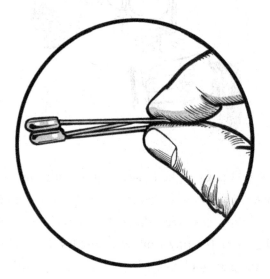

SECRET: It is best to use two larger safety pins, but any size will work. Hold the safety pins open, with both facing the same direction. Slyly place the pin end of safety pin A into the head—and closed position—of safety pin B. Then do the same with the pin end of safety pin B by placing it into the head of safety pin A. The crisscrossed pins will want to spring open, but a slight pinched grip holds them together, as shown above.

When people glance at the safety pins in this configuration, everything appears to be normal, as if one is resting on the other. Place the linked safety pins on the open palm of a spectator while keeping slight pressure on them, as shown in the second image. Ask the spectator to close his or her hand into a fist. After the spectator wraps his or her fingers around the safety pins, remove your fingers from the spectator's hand.

Make a magical gesture around the closed fist, or snap your fingers and say, "As you slowly open your hand, I will cause the safety pins to unlink!" At first the spectator will feel the safety pins coming apart, and then he or she will even hear the safety pins unlink. Any magician will tell you that some of the best magic happens in the spectator's hands.

It was my great-grandmother who showed me this trick.
She lived to be ninety-five, and she never used glasses.
She always insisted on drinking straight from the bottle.

Cellophane Surgery

The magician rips open the cellophane on the bottom of a borrowed pack of cigarettes. The magician rubs the torn pieces or allows someone else to rub the cellophane, and the plastic seals itself back to normal.

SECRET: Perform this effect with an open box of cigarettes wrapped in cellophane. Hold the box in your left hand. Discreetly, while talking to the spectators or misdirecting their attention, pull the cellophane wrapper about an inch off the box with your right hand, as shown in the top image. Give the wrapper a quarter turn, as shown in the second image. Then pull it flush against the bottom of the box, as shown in the third image. Fold the two protruding flaps down onto the bottom of the box, and hold them in place with the tip of your left index finger, as shown in the bottom image. Now that all looks normal, you are ready to present this little miracle.

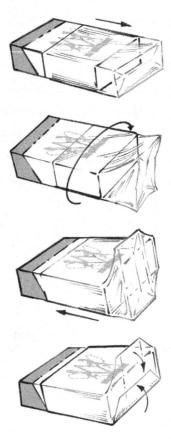

Ask the audience, "Have you ever heard of psychic surgery?" Add, "It was big in the Philippines for years. Basically, the surgeon would reach into patients' stomachs without making an incision, remove all the bad stuff, and seal them up without leaving a scar!" Say all this as you pick at the bottom of the cigarette box and apparently break the glue seal of the cellophane so that the flaps are protruding, as in the third image. Act as if this takes some effort, and milk the moment.

To apparently seal the cellophane back to new, all you have to do is turn the plastic wrapper a quarter turn in either direction and pull it down flush against the bottom of the box. To mask this action, turn the cellophane wrapper with your left hand's fingers while rubbing the bottom of the box with your open right hand. Better yet, have a spectator hold out a hand, palm-down. Then use one or both of your hands to turn the cellophane wrapper as you rub the bottom of the box in a circular motion against the spectator's palm.

When done, you can hand the box back to the spectator for examination. Say, "I've sealed it back better than new!" People are dumbfounded by this. This is the brainchild of a very clever magician from Hawaii named Allen Okawa and one of my favorite impromptu tricks to perform.

━━ ▭ ━━

If you are a smoker or know a smoker who is trying to quit, then let me tell you that according to a good friend of mine, the cigarette patch works. He put six of them over his mouth. Not only did he quit smoking, but he also lost weight.

CONVOLUTED COIN PREDICTION

The magician, in so many words, predicts the amount of change in someone's pocket.

SECRET: Write down this prediction for all to see:

I have as many coins as you, <u>3</u> more,
plus enough left over when added to your coins,
to give you a total of <u>37</u> coins.

This is a tricky way of saying that you have forty coins. It doesn't matter how many coins the other person has so long as it's less than you have. You can change the underlined numbers above so long as the two numbers equal forty. I carry eleven quarters, eight dimes, six nickels, and fifteen pennies in a small coin purse when I wish to perform this effect.

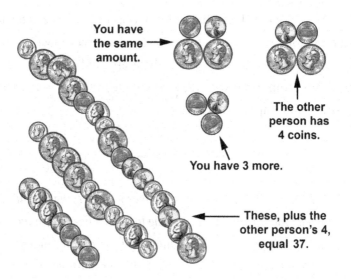

You have the same amount. →

The other person has 4 coins.

You have 3 more.

These, plus the other person's 4, equal 37.

PERFORMANCE: Place your fistful of forty coins next to your written prediction. Count out how many coins your volunteer has. Push them aside into a pile, and write that number down for all to see. Match that number of coins with your coins, and put them aside in a separate pile as you announce the quantity. Then blatantly place three coins in a third pile as you say, "Three more." Now, aloud, add your remaining coins to the volunteer's amount of coins, and it will total thirty-seven. You'll probably amaze yourself with this one!

This is an old trick that has evolved from magician to magician. One of the earliest versions with playing cards can be found in the 1938 book *Greater Magic* by John Northern Hilliard. This is one of my favorite bits of business.

─── ── ───

While this trick might not be a showstopper, I can
guarantee that it will slow it down a bit.

DEFACING A BILL

The magician rips out the portrait from a dollar bill and appears to eat this piece of the bill. The magician then pretends to spit it out toward the bill, and the dollar magically becomes whole again.

This is an abbreviated version of Rick Johnsson's "Dining on Dollars" trick, based on Jack Chanin's "Rip-It."

SECRET: Upon presenting this trick, say, "When I was kid, I had a bad habit of eating the faces from dollar bills!" Fold the length of a one dollar bill in half, and then tear the bill about a half inch below George Washington's portrait. Make another half-inch tear above the president's head. Hold the bill in your left hand, and make the tears with your right hand. The right thumb now folds this torn piece back behind the bill, and the left thumb holds the folded portrait in place, as shown above.

Pinch the middle of the portrait with your right index finger and thumb, and pull the pinched grip away briskly to make a ripping sound. Pinching the bill here should put a crease in the portrait to help it stay hidden behind the bill. Mime the action of holding a small piece of the bill in your right hand, and pretend to place it in your mouth. Act as if you're chewing and swallowing the piece, and say, "It's really good. You can taste the mint."

Grip the bill with your right hand while placing your left thumb between the ends of the bill, as shown in the second image. Grip the center end of the front of the bill with your left hand. Grip the center end of the back of the bill—the side facing you—with your right hand. The folded-over portrait should remain hidden and bent back toward you.

Say, "Of course it is illegal to deface government property," as you pretend to spit toward the bill. As you do this, pop open the bill to show the front to your audience, as shown in the third image. With your index finger and thumb's pinched grip at each end of the bill, pull on the dollar to make a crease down the length of the middle of the paper. This pulling action keeps the torn piece taut and flush with the rest of the bill. The camouflaged illusion is perfect.

——— —— ———

While keeping the dollar taut, casually show the back of the bill. Say, "I've found that the best way to double your money is to fold it in half and put it in your pocket," and do so.

Flying Pen Cap

As the magician pulls the cap off a Bic pen, it magically flies back on the pen.

SECRET: Use a Bic pen with a tapered cap. Hold the pen in your left hand, and remove the cap with your right hand in a pinched grip, as shown above. Very quickly move the cap around the head of the pen in a circular motion a few times, and pretend to build up some static electricity. To make the cap fly back on, squeeze or pinch the end of the cap firmly, and it will shoot from your fingers like a watermelon seed. Practice your aim so that it flies back on the pen. Pull the cap about an inch away, and snap the cap back on.

———

This is a great trick to show young people.
As a child is whirling the cap around the head of the pen,
smile and say, "I like you, kid. You remind me of myself
when I was young and stupid."

Book Test

The magician borrows two books and riffles through the pages of one of them. The spectator calls "stop" and turns to the same page in the other book. The magician has the spectator focus on the biggest word in the top line and reveals the word!

In the magic world, we call this a book test, where the magician reveals a random word from a book. Most book tests sell for hundreds of dollars or require some gimmick or setup. The beauty of this version, known as David Hoy's Bold Book Test, is that it can be performed impromptu with two borrowed books.

SECRET: Ask someone to loan you two books that are similar in size or page count. Pick up one of them and talk about it. You could talk about the title, the subject matter, whether you have heard of it or read it, etc. Make  small talk about the book while you casually flip through it. Discreetly glimpse the biggest word in the top line of one of the book's centermost pages and memorize the page number. This should be done without much hesitation. Let's call this book A.

After misdirecting the volunteer's attention away from your actions, ask him or her to choose a book. If the volunteer chooses book A, insist that he or she pick it up. Then riffle through the pages of book B and ask the volunteer to call "stop" at any time.

Typically, when you ask someone to call "stop," the person pauses about three seconds before saying, "Stop!" Time the action of riffling through the pages to stop near the center of the book. Open it up to the page the volunteer stopped at and miscall the number, giving the page number that you memorized the word for in book A. Then ask the volunteer to concentrate on the largest word in the top line, and do your best mind reader impersonation.

If the volunteer chooses book B in the beginning, ask him or her to hand it to you. This forces the person to take book A. This is better known as magician's choice or process of elimination. Then do the same trick.

It is best if you can sneak a peek at one of the books. Let's say you are at a friend's house, and the friend has some books on a coffee table. When the friend goes to the bathroom or to get a drink, glance at a page number and a word from one of the books on top of the pile. After some time has passed, tell the friend you'd like to try an experiment in ESP. Secretly use process of elimination to make sure that the book you've glanced at ends up in your friend's hands. You can then blow your friend's mind!

———

You could inquire, "Do you believe in ESP? You know, like when the phone rings and you know immediately who is calling. Oh, wait, that's Caller ID . . . that's not ESP."

FLOATING TO-GO CUP

A cup floats away from your hands while you hold it.

The next time you grab a cup to go, amaze your friends or onlookers by making it appear to float away from your grasp. The cup will seem to be lighter than air.

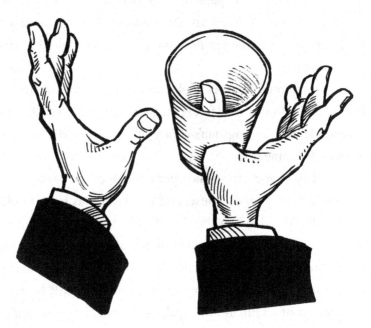

SECRET: The most common method uses an empty paper or Styrofoam™ cup. The magician silently and slyly pokes a hole in the back of the cup with one thumb and leaves it there. When the audience looks at it from the front, with your fingers spread wide, the cup appears to be floating, as shown above. Mime the action of having the cup rise away from you, and pretend to catch hold of it. Don't overdo it, or you might tip the method.

My friend, the brilliant author Martin Gardner, did some work on this old classic. Mr. Gardner placed a dab of rubber cement near the bottom of the cup and a little rubber cement on one of his thumbs. This allows the magician to touch the sticky tip of the thumb to the sticky portion of the cup and execute the same miracle. Instead of carrying a bottle of rubber cement with you, put some sticky dots in your wallet so that you can perform this trick seemingly impromptu. The bonus is that there is no hole in the cup when you are finished.

━━ ━ ━━

I love it when magicians come up with variations on tricks like this. I love magic—period. I remember, as a child, telling my mother that when I grew up, I wanted to be a magician. She replied softly, "Sweetie, I'm sorry to tell you that you can't do both."

Red & Black Prediction

The spectator mixes a deck of cards and separates the cards into three piles. The spectator is instructed to pull cards off the top of the deck, two at a time, and turn them faceup. The cards will be red-red, black-black, or red and black. The spectator places the pairs into one of the three piles, depending on the arrangement. The magician makes a prediction not once but twice before the spectator begins the procedure, and each time the magician predicts the outcome.

SECRET: This trick was first marketed as "Miraskill" by Stewart James in 1935. There are fifty-two cards in a normal deck—minus the jokers—with twenty-six red cards and twenty-six black cards. If someone follows the procedure, the red-red pile of cards and the black-black pile of cards will be even. To make it appear that this is not always the case, secretly remove four black cards from the deck and place them in the card box. Now you can predict that there will be four more red cards.

After you place the four black cards in the card box, hand the spectator the balance of the deck to mix. Explain how you would like the spectator to separate the cards into three piles, as explained above. Write down a prediction that says there will be four more red cards. After the spectator is done sorting the cards into piles, pick up the pile with the red and black cards and place them in the card box. Ask the spectator to count the pile of red cards and then the pile of black cards. Let's say there are twelve red cards and eight black cards. Ask the spectator to read your prediction aloud, and all will be impressed.

The kicker is doing it again! Remove all the cards from the card box—including the four black cards that were hidden inside—and ask the spectator to shuffle the cards again. While the spectator is mixing the cards, make another prediction that the red and black piles will be even. After going through the procedure of sorting the cards, the spectator will realize the different outcome, with both piles being equal.

——— —— ———

After reading your second prediction, the spectator will look at you starry-eyed and most likely ask you for the winning lottery numbers for that night. Remember that the definition of a lottery is a tax on people who are bad at math.

ONE DOLLAR PSYCHIC

Without seeing the front of a spectator's one dollar bill, the magician divines where the note was made!

Ask someone to take out a one dollar bill and find the black seal printed on the face of the note. This seal denotes which of the Federal Reserve Banks the bill is from. Insist that you do not want to see the front of the bill. Ask the person to study the back of the bill to verify that there are no indications of where it was made. Then concentrate and reveal the name of the Federal Reserve Bank where the bill was printed.

NOTES THE FEDERAL RESERVE BANK

SECRET: There are twelve Federal Reserve Banks in the US. Only one dollar bills spell out which of the twelve banks the bill was made at. There are eight places on the front of a bill where this is noted, as shown above. The obvious one is printed out in the lower portion of the black seal. Four are noted with a number (1 through 12). The last three are signified with a letter (A through L).

Memorize the list below or have a crib sheet handy to tell you which numbers and letters symbolize each Federal Reserve Bank.

1	A	Boston		7	G	Chicago
2	B	New York City		8	H	St. Louis
3	C	Philadelphia		9	I	Minneapolis
4	D	Cleveland		10	J	Kansas City
5	E	Richmond		11	K	Dallas
6	F	Atlanta		12	L	San Francisco

How do you know where the bill was printed if you never see the front? There are no indicators of the bank on the back. (If you look closely, you will find a small number underneath the big "E" in the word "ONE" on the back of the bill. This number only notes the placement of the bill on the sheet when it was made.)

When the person holds up the bill to look at the black seal, you can see through the bill in one clear spot, as shown on the previous page. This spot appears above the big "O" in "ONE" on the back of the bill. This magic spot shows a letter printed in dark green at the beginning of the serial number on the bill. That letter tells you which bank the bill was made at. If you don't glance at the letter through the bill when the person is studying the black seal, you'll have another chance when he or she puts the bill facedown on the table. You don't need much light to do this. In fact, you can do it with the bill flush on the table, with no light behind it.

A well-worn one dollar bill and a similarly distressed hundred dollar bill arrived at a Federal Reserve Bank to be retired. As they moved along the conveyor belt to be burned, they struck up a conversation. The hundred dollar bill reminisced about its travels. "I've had a pretty good life," the hundred proclaimed. "I've been to Las Vegas and Atlantic City, the finest restaurants in New York, and performances on Broadway and even on a cruise of the Caribbean." "Wow! You've really had an exciting life!" said the one dollar bill. "So tell me," said the hundred, "where have you been throughout your lifetime?" The one dollar bill replied, "Oh, I've been to the Methodist church, the Baptist church, the Lutheran church. . . ." The hundred dollar bill interrupted, "What's a church?"

The Missing Match

Lay out three similar matchbooks. Ask someone to remove a match from one of them and close the cover, all while your back is turned. Upon turning around and apparently weighing the matchbooks in your hand—or using psychic powers—divulge which matchbook the match was taken from.

SECRET: Without your audience knowing, make sure that all the covers are pushed in and locked tightly. When the volunteer removes a match and closes the cover, it will be the only matchbook with a loose cover. After you turn back around, hold each matchbook to your head, or pretend to weigh each one in your hand and gently press on each matchbook's cover. If the cover is tight, it is not the matchbook with the missing match. If the cover is loose, then you've got it.

——— —— ———

Most tricks or stunts are self-gratifying and are typically used to boost one's ego in a crowd. However, this stunt is sure to cause an audience to produce a huge round of indifference.

CONFEDERATE COASTERS

Nine coasters are placed in the formation of a square on the bar top. The magician turns his or her back to the group, and someone is asked to point at one of the coasters. Upon turning back around, the magician can always guess which coaster has been chosen.

SECRET: For this trick, you need a confederate. Your accomplice needs a drink and a coaster. While your back is to the audience and you are giving instructions to the spectators, your accomplice has a drink in hand. Once a coaster is chosen, your accomplice places the drink back on his or her coaster. Where on this coaster the accomplice places the drink is the key to telling you which coaster was chosen.

Imagine that your friend's coaster is a map divided into nine sections. If the center of the nine coasters is chosen, your accomplice places the drink on the dead center of his or her coaster. If someone chooses the upper-left coaster, your friend places the drink on the upper-left portion of his or her coaster, as shown on the facing page. And so on and so forth.

This is one of those effects that becomes increasingly amazing the more you do it. Sometimes people really buy into it, believe you have ESP, and ask you for a reading.

─── ▭ ───

When this happens, say, "I don't give readings, but I'd be happy to give you the number of a psychic friend of mine who gives personal consultations." Add, "I bet he'd even give you half off for reading your mind."

Penny Paradox

The magician makes four rows of pennies, each with four piles. Each row consists of ten coins. The magician asks someone to place another penny in any of the piles. After moving some of the coins around, the magician shows that there are still only ten coins in each row. Unbelievably, the magician does it again and again until the audience can take no more.

To perform this mathematical miracle, start with the coins in the configuration shown in the first image. Notice that there are four coins in opposite corners and three coins in opposite corners. In between each of the corners are two piles of coins consisting of three coins all together. The order of the middle piles doesn't matter so long as one pile has one coin and the other has two coins. Count the coins, and you will see there are ten coins in each row. Point out that you are counting the corners twice.

SECRET: If someone places a coin in a middle pile, make it vanish by moving one penny in a corner of the "same row" away from that row and into a middle pile. Look at the second image for an example of what to do. Now there are ten coins in each row again. Even knowing how this works, it seems incredible.

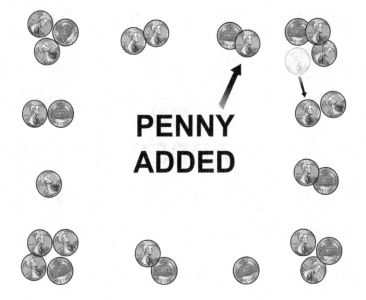

PENNY ADDED

This is easy to follow, so you should add many more penny switches to throw the audience off. You can move pennies in the center piles so long as the number of coins does not change quantities. Exchange a few coins in the center piles, do the secret move that matters, and then do a few more center pile switches. This makes the secret very difficult to discern.

If someone places a penny in a corner pile, there are eleven coins in two rows. To make ten coins in each row again, execute two secret moves. Follow the third image, and move one coin each from the two corners connected to the corner that the person added a penny to.

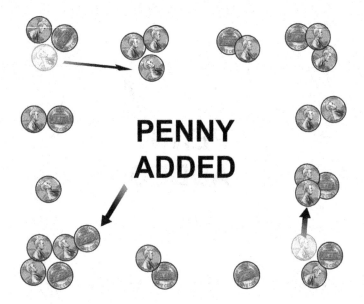

Never do the secret moves first. Do some of the center pile moves that cancel one another out, then the secret move, and follow it up with more center pile moves, which is really just a bunch of hokum. If the person puts a coin in a center pile, you have a choice of which corner to take from. It is always best to move a penny from a corner that has the most pennies. This allows you to continue the trick for some time.

You begin with twenty-six pennies. However, you can use matches, toothpicks, sugar packets, rocks, etc. I suggest doing this trick fast the first time. The next time, do it slower. The next time, push up your sleeves. The last time, after adding a penny, tell the audience which coins to move and never touch the coins. Stop the trick once one of the corners contains only one penny. Do the effect three or four times at most. It drives people insane. Have fun with it.

The best part is there is no sleight of hand. This is the most devious math trick I have ever found. The rumor is that this is an old con game that originated in India. The swindler would lay out coins placed on a handkerchief on a busy sidewalk. The swindler would then entice tourists to put a coin in a pile and apparently make it vanish. After doing this about ten times, the swindler would pick up the hanky full of money and go to another busy sidewalk to repeat the same con.

Do you know the best defense if ever attacked by a group of street performers? Always go for the juggler.

NAIL A NICKEL

The magician sticks a nickel to his or her forehead and, upon removing it, asks the spectator to try. When the spectator takes the nickel, all notice a nail sticking out from the back of it. Everyone can do nothing but laugh afterward.

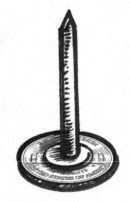

This is one of my favorite bits. I often use it as an opener when performing my strolling magic. The effect looks to be easy and ridiculous. As onlookers notice the nail on the back of the nickel, they think, "This guy is funny and full of surprises!"

SECRET: Take a small roofing nail, and superglue it to the back of a nickel, as shown above. Once dry, place the prepared nickel in your left pocket. Place a normal nickel in your right pocket. Begin the routine with both hands in your pockets in order to retrieve the nickels, and say, "Have you ever seen the world-famous nickel trick?" After waiting for a response, conclude, "It is one of the most difficult tricks that I perform." Now you've set the tone that the audience will see something impressive.

Bring forth the normal nickel in your open right hand. Remove the prepared nickel from your pocket with your left hand, and allow your left arm to relax at your side. All attention should be on the nickel in your right hand.

Press the back of the nickel in your right hand against the center of your forehead, and leave the coin there. The oil in your skin allows it to stay stuck to your head. Push the nail between the middle and ring fingers of your left hand. Allow your left thumb to rest on top of the head of the nickel to hold it in place. The left hand does this all at your side while out of the audience's line of sight.

Say, "Ladies love this trick," which is a bold statement. Continue, ". . . in India!" This causes most people to chuckle. Exclaim, "You should try it—it is harder than it looks," as you remove the coin from your head with your right hand. Place the normal nickel on your right hand's open fingers, and slowly raise your left hand from your side palm-down. To switch the nickels, place your right thumb on top of the nickel, and pretend to dump the coin in your open left hand as you turn it palm-up, as shown below. The illusion is perfect as the left hand's coin comes into view. Let your right arm fall naturally to your side so that it is out of sight and out of mind.

Say to someone, "Hold out your hand." As the volunteer reacts, secretly ditch the coin in your right hand into your lap while sitting or into your pocket if standing. Place the prepared nickel in the person's open hand nail side up. Make sure that he or she notices the nail by saying, "Be careful because it really hurts the first time!" Wince in pain, rub your forehead, and say, "Am I bleeding?" or "Did it leave a mark?" These statements are so silly that everyone is forced to laugh.

——— — ———

When somebody tries it, say, "Please be careful!
You might bend my nail."

COFFEE WRAPPER ILLUSION

An ordinary coffee cup wrapper is made to shrink and grow.

Coffee cup wrappers—holders, jackets, clutches, and sleeves—are the things used to insulate the cup and protect your hands from a hot drink. This trick works with most coffee shops' wrappers. This is an old optical illusion that requires two coffee cup sleeves.

SECRET: The trick works itself. If two paper insulators are placed on top of one another, they seem to be identical in size. However, if you place one below the other, it appears to grow in length.

When performing this optical illusion, ham it up by pretending to stretch or condense the paper with your magical powers. Perform this little miracle for someone, put one of the cup clutches on your drink, and walk away. With one cup sleeve left to examine, it is hard to figure out the mystery.

People have asked me if I wake up grumpy in the morning. I reply, "No. I bring her some coffee."

Sleight of Eye

The magician places a quarter in one of his or her eye sockets and then places open hands high into the air, as if surrendering to the police. The magician slowly turns around and faces the audience again. To everyone's amazement, the coin has vanished! The magician reaches up to the top of his or her head and produces the quarter for all to see.

SECRET: Wear a sport coat or at least a shirt with a breast pocket. Place something like a wadded-up tissue in your breast pocket to keep it open. When no one is looking, place a quarter on top of your head. Pull out another quarter, and call everyone's attention to your stunt.

Place the quarter in your eye socket that is above your breast pocket. Typically this is on the left side of your body. Shut your eyelid so that the coin doesn't touch your eye, and hold the coin there as if you are wearing a monocle. Throw your hands in the air, and slowly turn around. Once your back is to the audience, allow the coin to fall into your breast pocket. Practice the trick a few times to get your aim down; it can be learned quickly.

When you face your audience, people notice that the coin is no longer there. Allow the magic moment to sink in, and slowly remove the coin from atop your head and show it to everyone. Take a bow, and insist on applause. Unfortunately, if you are bald, you will not be able to hide the coin on top of your head.

━ ━ ━

However, if bald, you could teach the trick to a friend and use the top of your head to reflect the spotlight onto your friend for his or her shining moment!

Phone Number Trick

A volunteer is asked to enter his or her phone number in a calculator and multiply and add some other numbers to it. The magician figures out the phone number.

SECRET: After establishing yourself as an amazing entertainer, hand a calculator to a volunteer. Say, "I will make a prediction," as you scribble a big number in the millions on the back of a napkin (e.g., 11,541,704). Continue, "For this trick, we will use your phone number because there is no way I could possibly know that."

Instruct the volunteer to enter the first three digits of his or her cell phone number. Explain that you will not be using the area code. Ask, "What's the area code of your number?" If he or she replies, "214," say, "Okay. Don't put 214 in the calculator."

Make the volunteer aware that after each calculation, he or she should hit the equal button.

Step 1: Have the volunteer enter the first three digits of his or her cell phone number in the calculator.

Step 2: Ask the volunteer to multiply that number by 80.

Step 3: Ask the volunteer to add 1 to it.

Step 4: Tell the volunteer to multiply that by 250.

Step 5: Instruct the volunteer to add the last four digits of his or her number.

Step 6: Instruct the volunteer to add the last four digits of his or her number again.

Step 7: Tell the volunteer to subtract 250 from the total.

Step 8: Have the volunteer reveal your prediction! All will think that you have failed miserably.

Step 9: Take the calculator and divide the last number by two, and you will see the volunteer's phone number minus the area code. However, you already know the area code.

─── ── ───

Step 10: Whip out your cell phone, and call the number in front of everyone.

Numeration Revelation

Ask someone to concentrate on the last two digits of his or her birth year and add that two-digit number to the age he or she will be on his or her birthday in the current calendar year. The magician then reveals the secret number.

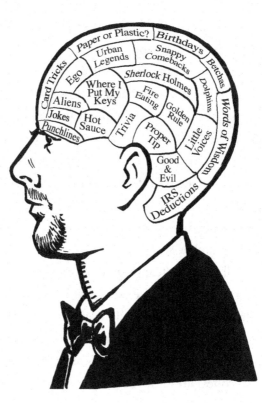

SECRET: This is something that is best done one-on-one because you don't want others to hear the answer. The answer is always 121 in 2021, 122 in 2022, 123 in 2023, etc. Basically, this is a tricky way of saying the year. If others hear you say this, they might deduce that it is always the same number for everyone. If no one else is around, the spectator surmises that the number is always unique.

There is an exception to this rule. Assuming you are reading this in the year 2021, anyone who was born before the year 2000 comes up with 121. Anyone born in 2000 or after comes up with 21. In 2022, the secret number will be 122 for those born before 2000 and 22 for those born in 2000 or after, and so on and so forth.

When presenting this little mystery, I prefer to work with an older person. It's more difficult to put together how you came up with the larger number 121 when using the year 2021.

You can really have some fun with this one. Rather than just blurting out the number, use your insight and tell spectators a little about themselves. Study their tea leaves. Bust out a crystal ball. Take a volunteer's hand and pretend to read his or her palm before revealing the number.

***

I'd recommend using the pseudoscience of phrenology, but people who believe in that should have their heads examined.

WATCH PREDICTION #2

The magician reveals a thought-of hour.

The magician writes down a prediction and folds it up to hide what has been written. The prediction is left in plain sight. The spectator is asked to look at any analog watch and think of an hour. The spectator should spell that hour beginning on one o'clock. For example, if the spectator thinks of five o'clock, he or she should spell "F-I-V-E," starting on one o'clock.

Whichever hour the spectator lands on, he or she should spell that number while beginning that word on the next hour. If the spectator lands on the number four, he or she should spell "F-O-U-R," beginning on five o'clock.

This leaves the spectator on a new number. Whatever that number is, have the spectator repeat the last step by spelling the hour he or she is on while starting on the next number in sequence. In our example, the new number is eight, so the spectator should spell "E-I-G-H-T" while starting on nine o'clock.

SECRET: Your written prediction should be one o'clock. If the spectator follows the directions, he or she always ends on one o'clock.

You can instruct the spectator to begin counting on twelve or one o'clock, and this still works. This effect comes from the creative mind of Jim Steinmeyer and was first published in his book *Impuzzibilities*.

——— ▭ ———

As the spectator opens your prediction to read it aloud, all should be enamored. To downplay this, I say, "Wow! I got it right. You know, even a broken clock is right twice a day."

Mental Monte

Three cards are shown faceup. A mark mentally selects one of them. While the magician faces the opposite direction, the cards are turned facedown and mixed. The magician turns back around and can guess the selection.

This trick was originally marketed by Bob Hummer as "Mathematical Three-Card Monte" in 1951. However, no math is used. The trick uses simple logic. Plus, it's unlike any other monte routine because the magician is looking for a thought-of card.

SECRET: Start by having three cards faceup on a table. They don't have to be playing cards. They could be coasters or business or index cards with messages written on them. The three things should be identical on one side, as with a standard playing card.

Ask someone to choose one of the cards mentally. Using the example shown above, pretend the mark has chosen the two of spades. It doesn't matter what he or she chooses; just remember the card on the far left: the ace of diamonds. Focus on that card. I choose the ace in this case because it is the only red card. Remember the ace's position, and turn around so that your backside is to the audience.

Ask the mark to turn the selected card facedown. Explain, "Now if I turn around, I'll know which card is yours, so turn the other two cards facedown and swap their two positions." Turn back around, and say, "Now obviously I can't know which card is yours," which is true, "but I'd like you to mix them further." As the mark mixes the cards, follow the card that you believe to be the ace of diamonds.

Once the mark finishes mixing the cards, pretend to read his or her aura, body language, or whatever mumbo jumbo you choose. The secret to knowing the card is simple. First, turn the card that you believe to be the ace of diamonds faceup. In our example, the card you're turning over is the three of clubs. Believe it or not, this tells you the identity of the chosen card.

By turning over the three of clubs, you know that the mark did not select the ace of diamonds, or it would've been there when you flipped it over. You know that it is not the three of clubs because that card was swapped with another. What remains is the two of spades, so that is the selected card.

After turning over the card you believe to be the ace of diamonds and learning that it is the three of clubs, you know that the mark chose the two of spades. After turning the first card faceup, turn over the other two cards. Study the cards for a moment, push the selected card toward the mark, and say, "This is the card you chose."

Some may think that it was luck or a one-in-three chance of success, so repeat the effect once or twice more. Let's say the cards are in the same order as shown in the image, and your back is to the audience. Ask someone to select a card and turn it facedown. Let's say he or she chooses the ace of diamonds. Be sure your instructions are clear: "Now turn over the other two cards, and swap their positions." If the mark mixes the cards at random, you'll have to be truly lucky or magical to find it.

Turn back around and mix the cards, or have the mark mix them. Keep track of the card you believe to be the ace of diamonds. Once the mixing has stopped, turn over the card you think is the ace, and in this case it will be. This tells you that the ace was chosen. Don't reveal the selected card until you've turned over the other cards and apparently studied them.

This simple bit of logic looks like true divination. The more you repeat the effect, the more impossible it seems. The clever mixing pattern is what allows you to know which card is chosen. The subtlety of turning around and continuing the mixing goes unnoticed by most laypeople.

The only way this trick can go awry is if you don't give good instructions. It's like Murphy's Law. Without proper guidance, anything that can go wrong will go wrong.

———— —— ————

Another thing to consider is Cole's Law.
Are you familiar with that? It's basically cabbage, carrots,
mayonnaise, and salt, all mixed together.

No-Tear Napkin

The magician rolls up a napkin and asks that the strongest person try to pull it in two. The volunteer can't do it. The magician puts a little muscle into it and shows that the outcome can be achieved.

Take a paper napkin, and twist it diagonally from corner to corner. Roll and pack it tightly. Hand it to someone, and ask the volunteer to attempt pulling it half. He or she will have no luck. Pass it around, and let others have a go at it.

SECRET: While everyone is taking a turn at it, secretly moisten the pads of your thumbs. When taking back the napkin, place your thumbs in the center of the napkin, as shown above. The moisture weakens the paper fibers and allows you to rip it into two pieces. Sometimes you have to rotate or twist the paper while tearing it.

This trick makes a good bar bet. Why not take a little money from your friends? What are friends for?

I made the mistake of lending a friend of mine $1,000 for plastic surgery once, and now I can't recognize him to get my money back.

Psychokinetic Paper Clip

The magician asks a volunteer to straighten a paper clip to the best of his or her ability. The magician takes the straightened paper clip and holds it at his or her fingertips. While onlookers gaze upon it, and the magician's every move, the paper clip bends right before their eyes.

SECRET: The paper clips should be about two inches long before being straightened. Once the paper clip is straightened, it is about six inches long. A volunteer should straighten the paper clip so that the audience knows how difficult it is to bend—or at least realizes that it takes some effort. No matter how hard the volunteer tries to straighten the paper clip, it will still have a few kinks in it, which helps with the illusion. As you take back the straightened paper clip in your right hand, hold it as shown below.

Your right hand's thumb and fingers should put an extreme bend in the paper clip about two inches from the end. This action is shielded by your right hand's curled fingers. Adjust your grip so that you hold the paper clip by each end with each hand. Imagine that the warped paper clip is lying flat on a table, and hold it in that fashion. The bend will be undetectable to onlookers so long as you keep it at their eye level. If spectators can look up or down at the warped paper clip, they will see that it is bent.

Let go of the end of the paper clip with your left hand, and hold the tip of the opposite end with your right index finger and thumb. Pretend to concentrate your energy on the paper clip, and gesture with your left hand near the clip. Hold your left hand flat several inches above the paper clip's bend, extend your middle finger down, and wiggle it as you slowly rotate the paper clip downward with your right thumb and index finger, as shown below. Done slowly, this looks creepy, as if the paper clip is bending right before people's eyes. Once the paper clip is extremely bent, hand it to a spectator as a souvenir. Add, "Notice it is still bending." Those who choose to believe it will.

Afterward, pretend to be dizzy. Say, "Whoa! I just had an out-of-body experience. I was beside myself."

Newspaper Numbers

The magician asks someone to choose any section from a newspaper (e.g., editorial, front section, international news, sports, entertainment, classified ads, comics). The magician asks the spectator to remove any four-page spread and add the four page numbers. The magician divines the sum.

SECRET: This is a great routine that can be done impromptu. The only thing you need is a newspaper that has a traditional four-page layout. After the spectator chooses a section, take hold of it. Tell the spectator to remove any four-page spread from that section and add up the four page numbers. Pantomime this action to be clear. The numbers to be added are the inside page numbers and the two found on the back of the same sheet.

As soon as you have the section in your hands, it is easy to divine the sum. Add the numbers on the front and back of the first page. The front-page number might be 1, and the back-page number might be 40. Adding those two numbers together gives you 41. Multiply that number by 2, and you get the final result, 82. If the front and back pages are 1 and 40, which total 41, then on the opposite sides are 2 and 39, which total 41 again. 41 multiplied by 2 is 82. Every four-page spread in that section adds up to 82.

It only takes a moment to glance at the back-page numbers and do the math. This trick could also be done with a book. The problem with a bound book is that one cannot easily remove a four-page spread. If you remove the staples from a saddle-stitch book, you can perform the same miraculous effect.

Once upon a time, a good friend gave me a beautiful
antique dictionary. The binding came undone over time,
and several pages fell out and were lost. You know,
I couldn't find the words to thank him.

VORTEX MOVE

A bent card stands upright on a tabletop. It falls over after the magician shoots it with an imaginary gun.

This trick uses what I named the "vortex move" and was first published in *Genii* magazine in 2000. The original effect makes a card an inch or two away from the magician fall over. The principle can be extended to make a card fall over when it is several feet away. I've performed this trick across an eight-foot pool table. My idea was to turn the backhanded motion to look like a magician is drawing a gun and then turning his or her fingers into a gun to shoot the card dead.

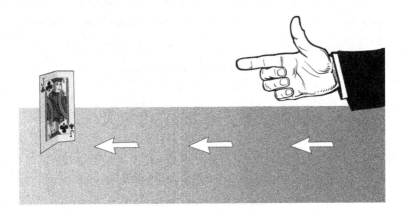

SECRET: Bend a playing or business card lengthwise from edge to edge, putting a natural bow in it. Do not crease it. Place the card upright on a counter or tabletop a few feet away. Make sure there is a clear path between you and the card. Stand near the edge of the table, which should be about waist level, and place your hands naturally at your side.

To execute the vortex move, use your right hand, pretending to draw an imaginary gun from your left side. Keep your right hand's fingers straight, and swiftly move your right hand toward the tabletop. Stop suddenly several feet away once your hand is in perfect alignment with the card. Quickly, make a gun with your right hand and pretend to shoot the card, as shown on the facing page. Once the card begins to fall over, mimic the action of the gun's recoiling with your right hand. Afterward, pretend to blow away the smoke from the barrel of the gun; this subtlety brings your hand closer to you, emphasizing the magic.

Practice this move until you can do it every time. Make sure you do not touch the tabletop. You don't want anyone thinking you jarred it. Emphasize that your hand is several feet away from the card. The card appears to fall over seconds after your hand has ceased moving.

A variation of this effect is to put a beer or wine bottle between your hand and the card. The vortex of air moves around it. You could also put a lit tealight on the tabletop with a bottle in front of it and then use the vortex move to extinguish the flame.

The first trick in my book *Close-Up Magic Secrets*, also published by Dover Publications, is titled "Gunslinger" and features the vortex move. Not only does the card fall over dead in the routine, but a bullet hole appears in the signed card as well.

———

The book you are reading now is my sixth book. I like to think that everyone is entitled to my opinion.

Toxic

A spectator multiplies some numbers together in a smartphone's calculator, and the magician predicts the outcome.

SECRET: Borrow someone's smartphone, and access the calculator app. Without letting the spectator see your actions, hit "C" or "AC," which stands for "clear" or "all clear," to erase any past calculations. Then enter whatever you would like your force number to be (e.g., 3,975,864). Hit the plus sign, then 0, then the multiplication sign. Just remember +0x, which looks like the first three letters of the word "toxic." This secretly hides the force number until someone hits the equal symbol.

When this was taught to me, I was told to enter +0x and then (, which is the open parenthesis symbol and corresponds to "C" in "toxic." To enter the (symbol, you need a scientific calculator. Most smartphone owners don't know that if they turn a smartphone sideways, the calculator app switches to scientific mode. However, one doesn't need to enter the (symbol for the magic to work. Ask a mathematician, but it has something to do with the order of operations or some mumbo jumbo.

Once you've entered your force number, return the phone to its owner. Your stated reason for borrowing the phone was to pull up the calculator app and make sure it was cleared out before the procedure. You know that the calculator app is ready because the multiplication symbol is highlighted in white.

Write down your force number on a piece of paper, calling it a prediction. Fold up the paper, and ask someone to hold on to it. Using the spectator's calculator, ask him or her to enter any three-digit number and hit the multiplication symbol. Ask the spectator to repeat the previous action. For the third time, ask him or her to enter a three-digit number and press the multiplication symbol. Then ask the spectator to hit the equal symbol. Your force number should pop up on the screen.

Ask the spectator to open and read your prediction aloud, and all will be astonished by your wizardly ways. Guide the spectator every step of the way so that he or she doesn't hit the equal button too early. If the spectator hits the equal button after each calculation, the trick does not work. When multiplying three different three-digit numbers together, the result is always in the millions, so the suggested prediction of 3,975,864 seems copacetic.

It doesn't matter if you add some operations to your instructions. The spectator could add or subtract too. Don't include any division because you don't want any of the working numbers to have decimal points, or else the revelation will look bogus. The entry numbers could have two, three, or four digits. Just make sure that the force number looks realistic. You could also use the force number to reveal a personal number like a birthday or phone number.

Once you have entered the force number in the calculator app, the only telltale sign of foul play is the multiplication symbol, which is highlighted in white. There is a solution that removes the highlight. After entering the force number, hit the +0x buttons, and then hit 0. Proceed with the effect, and all will work just as smoothly.

I must reiterate the importance of guiding the spectator during the entry of the numbers and calculations. If the trick goes wrong, it is your fault. In this ADD culture we live in, you must insist on the spectator's full attention.

I myself have HDADD; that's High-Definition Attention Deficit Disorder. I have trouble paying attention, but when I do, it is extremely clear.

Raising Raisins

Drop a raisin in beer, and it will fall to the bottom of the glass and then float up to the top. Once it is on top, it will fall back to the bottom and repeat the cycle.

SECRET: This works because carbon dioxide bubbles in the beer cling to the surface of the raisin. Once the surface of the raisin accumulates enough bubbles, it floats up. When the raisin rises to the top, the bubbles are released and pop, and gravity pulls the raisin back down. This cycle typically repeats itself for a while. For fun, drop a few raisins in your beer and enjoy the show.

If you are not a beer drinker, you can perform this stunt with ginger ale. Supposedly, ginger ale can be used to clean up your clothing if you spill your drink on yourself. But what does one use to get ginger ale out of clothing? This is the same dilemma as "What does one use after spilling carpet cleaner on a carpet?"

Pasteboard Psychic

The magician calls a friend and asks him or her to find a deck of cards and shuffle it. The friend cuts the deck into three piles. The piles are reassembled, and the deck is shuffled with some cards faceup and some facedown. The friend sorts the cards into faceup and facedown piles while calling out all the faceup cards. Once the spectator finishes sorting the pack, the magician identifies the selected card.

This is a classic among magicians, but the creator is unknown. It was first advertised in *The Sphinx* in the 1930s. It was made popular by the great Eddie Fields. It is a wonderful effect. How many card tricks do you know that you can do over the telephone or internet without video?

ROUTINE: Call a friend, and ask him or her to find a deck of cards. It doesn't matter if the deck is missing a few cards. Ask the friend to shuffle the deck just in case the cards are in order. The friend should cut the deck into three approximately equal facedown piles, as shown above. He or she should pick up a pile, remove a card, and memorize it or write it down. The friend should put the chosen card facedown on top of the pile he or she took it from.

Tell the friend to turn that pile faceup and place it on top of one of the facedown piles. The friend should pick up the remaining facedown pile and drop it on top of the other cards. There should now be a bunch of faceup cards sandwiched between a bunch of facedown cards. The friend should cut the deck in half and shuffle the two halves together, which creates a slew of integrated faceup and facedown cards.

Instruct the friend to sort the cards into faceup and facedown piles by dealing them off the top of the deck. Ask him or her to call out each faceup card.

SECRET: As the friend calls out the faceup cards while sorting them, listen to the name of each card. Eventually the friend will name a card, and afterward there will be a long stretch of facedown cards. While he or she is sorting and dealing the facedown cards, there is a long pause before there's another faceup card. The long pause tells the magician that the card that came immediately before it was the selected card.

Wait until the friend has sorted all the cards before naming the selected card. Ham it up, and do your favorite mind-reading bit.

——— ▭ ———

Speaking of mind reading, did you hear about the two
psychics who bumped into each other on the street?
One said, "You're fine. How am I?"

1089

Someone jots down a thought-of three-digit number. More numbers are subtracted and added, yet the magician can always predict the outcome.

Have someone write down a three-digit number where the ones digit is small, the middle digit is larger, and the remaining digit is the largest, like 962.

Ask the volunteer to reverse the number, write it underneath, and subtract the smaller number from the larger one. Whatever the result is, ask the volunteer to write that number backward under the third number. Instruct him or her to add the last two three-digit numbers together.

SECRET: The result is always 1089.

Hand the volunteer paper to work out the calculations. Before he or she begins, rip off a piece of the paper, secretly write 1089 on it, and crumple the paper into a ball to hide the message.

After giving the above instructions and before opening the ball of paper, wave your hand magically over the wad and exclaim, "I'll use the magic word I learned in church. . . ."

As the audience ponders what blasphemous thing you're about to say, open the crumpled ball for all to read.
Say, "Bingo!"

COIN ILLUSION

The magician causes the image of a gray coin to appear inside a hypnotic circle printed on a small piece of paper. The magician shakes the paper, and a real coin flies out.

SECRET: The hypnotic circle shown above is an old optical illusion. If you move the figure in a circular motion very quickly, a small gray circle or coin-like object appears to be rolling inside the circle and along the outside border of the image. The 3-by-3-inch dimensions of the image above produce the illusion of a coin the size of a quarter.

When showing someone this book or a photocopy of the above image, hide a quarter in your hand and load it underneath the book or paper. Briskly whirl the image around in a clockwise or counterclockwise motion a few times until the onlooker claims to see the coin. Once he or she confirms the illusion, give the book or paper a little shake and let the quarter fly toward them. You could catch the coin in your other hand or have a spectator hold out his or her hands to receive the quarter, as shown below. This looks very magical!

When introducing the piece of paper with the hypnotic circle, say, "Here's a little trick I picked up. I don't know who dropped it."

CALLING MR. WIZARD #3

Someone is asked to name any playing card aloud and then use his or her cell phone to call your friend Mr. Wizard. Upon answering, Mr. Wizard reveals the thought-of card.

This is my favorite adaptation of this effect, which was invented by Australian magician Tim Ellis. The trick's original title is "Cellular Thinking."

SECRET: When you have some privacy, dial Mr. Wizard and tell him that you are about to perform this effect. Without disconnecting the call, put the phone in your pocket. A shirt pocket or jacket breast pocket is best. Now your phone is acting like a walkie-talkie that is constantly on. Before approaching a group, I sometimes embellish the effect by telling Mr. Wizard a little about the person who is about to think of a card. I tell Mr. Wizard what the person is wearing, his or her hair color, whether or not the person is wearing glasses, and something personal if I have that information.

With your phone on, ready, and hidden, ask someone to think of a card and name it aloud. If you think Mr. Wizard didn't hear the card called, repeat it by saying, "Okay, the three of clubs." As soon as Mr. Wizard hears the card, he should hang up. Instruct someone to call your psychic friend Mr. Wizard with his or her phone and ask if he can reveal the card the person is thinking of. When Mr. Wizard reveals things about the volunteer and his or her thought-of card, everyone should be impressed. This effect makes a wonderful closer because it is so powerful.

Typically, audience members look around the room to see who is helping you or if someone might have overheard what was said. They never find an accomplice. Do not use your phone when calling Mr. Wizard. Insist that the volunteer call on his or her own phone.

——— —— ———

I tell my audience that if they want to keep guys like Mr. Wizard and me from reading their minds, they should try wrapping tin foil around their heads to help jam the brain wave frequencies that they are emitting.

Ticktock Telekinesis

A volunteer's borrowed watch moves forward in time while he or she holds it.

A variation of this trick was published in *The Ganson Book* by Lewis Ganson and is accredited to Martin Breese. Today most magicians associate it with the mentalist known as Banachek. The effect is a reputation-maker that leaves audiences dumbstruck. In my humble opinion, it is one of the most powerful impromptu magic effects ever devised.

SECRET: Scour the crowd, and pay close attention to the types of watches people are wearing. The method for this effect does not work with digital watches. It's best not to use watches with multiple stems or buttons to adjust the time or date. Borrow a watch that only has one stem, as most analog watches do.

When you spot the appropriate watch, ask to borrow it. Once the volunteer removes the watch, hold it with your right hand and ask the audience to note the time. Notice the position of your right hand's middle finger. As you bring the watch up near your chest to read the time aloud, your right middle finger should secretly pull out the stem of the watch.

Use your right index finger to roll the stem under the watch and toward your body, as shown on the facing page. This causes the watch to move forward in time. Secretly push the stem back in the watch. Make a mental note of the new time on the watch.

The above actions are done quickly and under the guise of misdirection. It should take five seconds or less to change the time on the watch. Once you complete the covert actions, slide your fingers toward the end of each band and hold them there. This is the mental picture that you want your audience to remember.

While holding the watch by the strap ends, ask onlookers if they believe in telekinesis or if they've ever read *The Time Machine* by H. G. Wells. Discuss something that has to do with altering time, and ask the volunteer to hold the watch between the palms of his or her hands. Carefully, place the watch in the volunteer's hand facedown to hide the time change. After your intelligent discussion, explain that you will attempt to move the minute hand of the watch forward. Wave your hands over the volunteer's hands, and do your best Uri Geller impersonation.

While waving your hands, ask, "Did you feel anything?" Usually the volunteer responds "No," but once in a while, he or she says "Yes." Pull your hands away, and proclaim, "I think I've done it! I believe I've moved the minute hand forward about X minutes." X equals the number of minutes you noted earlier when secretly adjusting the time. Demand that the volunteer read the time aloud as you back away. Everyone's reactions should be priceless.

There are many scientists who believe that time is merely an illusion. I'm not sure about that. However, I do know that time is what keeps everything from happening all at once.

Spirited Dime

The magician places a dime atop the mouth of an empty glass bottle. The magician places his or her hands on the bottle and concentrates. Suddenly, the dime comes alive and bounces up and down on the bottle.

SECRET: You must use a dime for this effect because other coins are too heavy. Select a glass beer or Coke® bottle where the dime completely covers the mouth of the bottle. Use a bottle that has been recently emptied so that it still has a little condensation inside. It helps if the mouth of the bottle is wet.

To make the dime move, wrap your hands around the body of the bottle, as shown above. Your body warmth heats the bottle. The heated bottle warms the liquid, creating combustion. The combustion tries to escape the bottle time and again, which makes the dime bounce up and down. The warmer your hands are, the faster this works.

When done right, this can be a spooky sight to behold. This effect could cause chills to run up people's spines.

If that doesn't work, have a friend jump into the room wearing a full-face mask made of lunch meat and watch them scatter!

Ticket to Heaven

The magician folds and tears a piece of paper while telling a story of three men's journey to heaven. At the end of the story, the pieces of paper reveal a moral to the story.

SECRET: Take a piece of standard 8.5 x 11 paper. The size of the paper does not matter, but the paper must be rectangular. Take the top right corner of the paper and fold it down, as shown in the first image. Fold the top point or left corner of the paper down, as shown in the second image. Now fold the paper in half or over on itself, as shown in the third image. Think of it as the first three folds when making a small paper airplane glider.

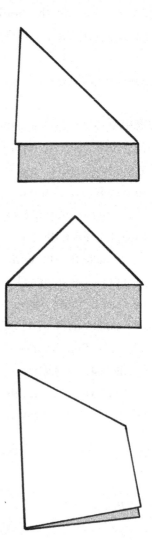

Hold the paper on the longest side, with your right hand, and visualize three equally wide sections, as shown in the fourth image. Tear the paper into those sections as straight as possible. The longest piece goes into your shirt pocket. Place the remaining pieces on the table. Tell the following story while performing the folding and tearing actions.

The story goes that a good man dies and is given a ticket to heaven. While waiting for his plane ride to that nirvana in the sky, he folds up the ticket to make a paper plane as he ponders his childhood. He begins thinking about birthdays, holidays, vacations, the loved ones he left behind, and those he will soon be reunited with. Eventually he grows weary while waiting and places the folded ticket in his pocket before taking a little nap.

Two bad men, who are ticketless, notice the sleeping man and see their chance to sneak onto the plane to heaven. One of the bad men slyly removes the ticket from the good man's pocket and tears off a piece for himself. He tears off a piece for his partner in crime. He then puts the remaining piece—the larger one—back in the sleeping man's pocket.

Later they all hop on the plane and arrive at the pearly gates. The angel taking tickets stops the two bad men once he sees their torn pieces of ticket. He says, "I'm sorry. There's only one place that you can get into with this. Let me spell it out for you." The angel spells out the word "HELL." (Use the pieces on the table to form the word, as shown below. It becomes obvious how to do it after a couple of practice rounds.)

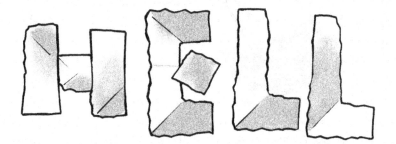

The conscience of one of the bad men gets the better of him, and he exclaims, "I feel bad because I tore up the ticket of a perfectly good and innocent man, and now he can't get into heaven either." The angel replies, "Don't worry about him. He's already been taken care of." This last statement is made as you unfold the bigger piece that was in your pocket. It forms the shape of a cross.

This may sound corny, but audiences act amazed upon seeing how perfectly the pieces form the word "hell" and make a cross. Some people are very moved. Embellish the story to suit you.

———

Always remember that God is watching us
so you might as well be entertaining.

ABOUT THE AUTHOR

Diamond Jim Tyler has practiced magic since he was five years old and performed it professionally since 1986. DJT is the creator of dozens of effects sold worldwide and the author and publisher of several best-selling magic books, including *Close-Up Magic Secrets* and *Bar Bets to Win Big Bucks*, both published by Dover Publications. He has contributed to several magic publications, and his routines are performed by magicians all over the world.

DJT's act has been featured at the Improv; the Magic Castle in Hollywood, California; and The Magic Circle in London. He has performed in forty-eight states in the US and twenty-nine other countries as well as on TV shows like *Dude Perfect*. He has received awards from The International Brotherhood of Magicians and the Texas Association of Magicians. DJT is also a Guinness World Records holder.

DJT headlines conventions globally, teaching other magicians his routines. He has entertained celebrities such as Jon Bernthal, Matt Damon, Jason Derulo, Leonardo DiCaprio, DJ Khaled, Colin Farrell, Jeff Goldblum, Scarlett Johansson, John Legend, Jay Leno, John Mayer, Bob Odenkirk, Aaron Paul, Katy Perry, Chrissy Teigen, and Dick Van Dyke. Plus, he's a regular guest star on the online show *Scam Nation*, which has almost two million followers!

To learn more about his adventures, watch video demonstrations, and see his full line of magic products, visit www.djtyler.com.